The Perfect Shot: Mini Edition for North America II

Shot Placement for Bear, Bison, Cougar, Goat, Hog, Javelina, Muskox, Sheep, & Wolf

by
CRAIG T. BODDINGTON

Artwork by
LAURIE O'KEEFE

T0164101

ACKNOWLEDGMENTS

The author would like to acknowledge that excerpts were taken from *American Hunting Rifles,* his previous North American book by Safari Press.

The publisher would like to thank the following photographers for the use of the photos seen throughout this book and on the cover: Dusan S. Smetana, Gary Kramer, Len Rue Jr., Leonard Lee Rue III, Charles J. Alsheimer, George Barnett, John Ford, and Michael Francis.

****

Boddington, Craig T.
O'Keefe, Laurie
First edition
Safari Press Inc.
2009, Long Beach, California
ISBN 1-57157-330-5
Library of Congress Catalog Card Number: 2004091079
10 9 8 7 6 5 4 3 2
Printed in China
Readers wishing to receive the Safari Press catalog, featuring many fine books on big-game hunting, wingshooting, and sporting firearms, should write to Safari Press Inc., P.O. Box 3095, Long Beach, CA 90803, USA. Tel: (714) 894-9080 or visit our Web site at www.safaripress.com.

TABLE OF CONTENTS

INTRODUCTION

I wish I could lay claim to the brilliant insight that has resulted in the publication of what has become a series of Perfect Shot books from my old friends at Safari Press. Unfortunately I cannot. Credit for the genesis of the idea must go to another friend and colleague, Kevin Robertson, who conceived *The Perfect Shot: Africa,* and to our publisher, who decided the concept needed to be expanded into a North American version, and then miniaturized into a handy field edition.

This has been done. However, the initial publication of *The Perfect Shot: Mini Edition for North America,* in order to keep it "mini," focused on the game animals that are probably most familiar to the majority of North American hunters. The book (or, properly, "booklet") is thus extremely useful, but also incomplete. In this companion volume, then, you will find the North American game animals that, because of habitat and opportunity, are probably somewhat less familiar to most hunters. Since many of the animals covered herein will be less familiar to many of us, this little book may well be of greater value than the mini edition that preceded it. At least I hope so, because that is its intent! Again, I wish I could say this was my great idea, but over the years I've learned that Ludo Wurfbain and his Safari Press team are far better at good ideas than I will ever be! The good news it that I've also learned that when they have ideas, I better listen!

Shot placement is, of course, of paramount importance no matter what the game, and with Laurie O'Keefe's wonderful artwork, that question will be answered. But most of us, including me, have interests beyond the mere placement of the shot, whether we have the opportunity to hunt these animals or not. I hope the brief notes on rifles, cartridges, bullets, hunting techniques, good areas, and more will also be of interest, will answer questions, and undoubtedly will stir campfire discussions. Because, after all, the ideas in this book are mine, and don't necessarily have to be yours.

So when we meet around a campfire, please bring out your dog-eared copy of *The Perfect Shot: Mini Edition for North America II*, and bring my attention to one page or another. I'm sure we'll have a lot to talk about. In the meantime, good luck, good hunting, and may your shots always be more perfect than mine.

Craig Boddington
Paso Robles, California
April 2008

The point of aim for the heart, lung, and shoulder shots is indicated. Although the black bear is, on average, not any heavier than a whitetail, its bones and muscle mass are certainly a lot tougher. (Photo courtesy of Len Rue Jr.)

BLACK BEAR
Don't underestimate him!

The black bear, *Ursus americanus*, is found discontinuously from Southern California to Newfoundland and from Florida to Alaska. Although the black bear is primarily a creature of the forests, it is extremely adaptable, as its huge range suggests. The black bear is found in southern swamps, northern hardwood forests, well out into the tundra of Canada and Alaska, the rain forests of the Pacific Northwest, and throughout virtually every mountain range from Mexico to Canada. This last includes the arid mountains of the Southwest.

It's hard to say exactly where black bear cannot survive, but at this writing the only habitat types that black bear don't inhabit are open plains and true deserts. But they'll be nearby. In the Great Plains you don't find black bear in the open grasslands, but you find them in appropriate habitat close-by, such as the Black Hills. You also don't find black bear on the sunbaked floor of any desert—but look around in the surrounding mountains, and if there's sufficient water, there will probably be bear.

Coast to coast, and in all record-keeping systems, there is just one black bear. Not all black bear are black, however. There are many color phases, with the most common variations some shade of brown. The "brown black bear" ranges from blond to very red, but dark brown is the most common. Color phases do follow regional patterns. Most of the bear in the East are black, often with a white patch on the brisket. Bear in the Pacific Northwest

An ideal shot on a mature, good-size black bear. For a shot like this, a premium, well-constructed bullet is not needed. Then again, in another ten seconds an entirely different picture may present itself; therefore, well-constructed bullets are good to have. (Photo courtesy of Len Rue Jr.)

are usually black, but along the Rocky Mountains brown bear are quite common—in some areas more common than black bear.

There are also a couple of localized rarities. The "glacier bear" or "blue bear" is an extremely unusual color phase of the black bear, with varying degrees of white hair in the coat. At a distance this gives the bear a very blue appearance. The glacier bear is known to occur only in southeastern Alaska, generally in the Yakutat area. Rarer still is the Kermode bear, the "white black bear." Known to occur only in British Columbia's Queen Charlotte Islands, the Kermode bear is ghostly white, but it has black eyes and dark claws, so it is not an albino. This color phase is completely protected.

There are several principles that generally hold true with all the color phases. First, the lighter-colored bear are generally small and young, so very big blond bear are rare. The beautiful light reddish-brown "cinnamon bear" are usually not the biggest bear, and the really silvery glacier bear are also usually small. Second, brown sows can have black cubs, and vice versa. I once saw a glacier bear sow with two small cubs that were coal black. The color of the cubs depends on the genes carried by the sow and boar. The colors must be in the local gene pool in order to occur at all, and black is probably dominant in most areas. Finally, bear do change color as they mature. Usually the shift is from light to dark.

I shot that big midnight-blue bear, certain I had found a monstrous glacier bear. It died in a thick patch of cover, and when guide Jack Ringus and I approached it, I was crestfallen. It was big, but it looked like—well, like a black bear. Then the sun came out

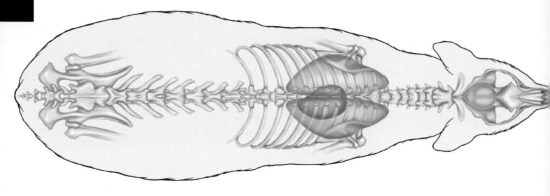

Notice how the lungs of a black bear are in a more forward position than those of a deer. Also keep in mind that if a bullet or arrow hits the spine from a top-angle shot like this one, a lot of tough material needs to be penetrated before the projectile will reach the heart/lung area.

and it turned blue. We looked carefully, and its generally black fur had an underlayer of white hairs on shoulders, flank, and hips. In sunlight it appeared blue, but in shadow the black completely overpowered the white underlayer. This was an old bear, and one might theorize that, in its younger days, it was very gray. A glacier bear in the Anchorage Zoo was much the same; it started out gray-blue but became very dark as an old bear.

Color phases don't vary in all areas, but body size does. Body size depends largely on food, genetics, and the opportunity to mature and reach maximum size. Remote areas like Newfoundland and Vancouver Island are known to produce numbers of very large black bear—but so are strange places like Arizona's San Carlos Reservation, western Pennsylvania, and North Carolina's Lake Mattamuskeet. This suggests that a really big black bear could occur almost anywhere bear are found, and I believe this to be true.

And that's one of the big problems with hunting black bear. The average black bear is not a large animal. Body weight of about two hundred pounds is normal for a grown-up black bear almost anywhere, especially in the spring when the bear have just come out of hibernation and body fat is depleted. This doesn't mean the black bear should be taken lightly; I know three experienced black bear guides who were severely mauled by "small" black bear in this class. However, black bear do get bigger—a lot bigger.

Bear have especially keen ears and noses but a limited ability to see. If a bear gets your scent, the hunt is over, but if the wind is right and you are quiet, bear are extremely "stalkable," even if you don't have a completely covered approach. Mind you, they are not blind. It's

Most black bears are similar in size to a large deer; however, the construction of the bullet needs to be more robust than that for a deer. (Photo courtesy of Len Rue Jr.)

always better to stay out of sight, but if you stay off the skyline and move slowly, you can approach a bear within fairly short rifle range. Bow range is more difficult, but even that is much more possible than with any horned or antlered game.

Shots at Black Bear

The kind of shot you get depends on the hunting technique you use. There are three primary options, and they vary depending on the country and also on the local tradition. Perhaps the oldest technique is hunting bears with hounds. This was the way Daniel Boone and Davy Crockett hunted their bears, but hound hunting has come under heavy fire from antihunters who call it "unsporting"; it's been outlawed in many areas. Hound hunting is the most selective of all bear-hunting techniques. Bear are very hard to judge, but in hound hunting you have two exceptional opportunities. The first occurs when you find the track. If it isn't a big track, or if tracks of cubs are in evidence, you simply find another track. The second occurs at the tree. You will almost always get a close-range look at your bear, and there is absolutely no reason to make a mistake or to shoot a bear you don't want.

In hound hunting the range will be very short, sometimes a matter of feet but rarely more than a few yards. Hound hunting is a business of following the music of the pack, keeping up with the chase no matter how rough or thick the country, and then getting to the tree before the bear gets a second wind and starts the chase all over again. The shooting will be very simple and somewhat anticlimactic . . . provided you do it right. If you don't, then you

The Perfect Shot: Mini Edition for North America II

have a wounded and enraged bear on the ground at close range, an immediately dangerous situation for your canine hunting companions and potentially hazardous for you as well.

Baiting is another traditional hunting method, generally practiced in thickly forested areas where visibility is limited. It is extremely effective, for the key to a bear's heart is its stomach. In the spring, after a long winter's nap, bear are ravenous and will bait readily. This method is less reliable in the fall, but as the bear try to pick up body fat in preparation for winter, they can definitely be baited. It isn't quite as easy as it sounds; consistently baiting trophy-class bears is almost an art form. Every old bear hunter has his favorite bait. Some use meat, some use fish, and some use sweets like stale donuts or a homemade molasses brew.

I'm not sure the actual bait matters so much, but exactly where the bait is sited and how the blind is set up matter a great deal. Over a bait the location of the blind absolutely controls the shot. Bow hunters usually site a tree stand no more than thirty yards away. This is really too close, not only because of scent but also because any movement at all is likely to spoil the show. Most rifle hunters place blinds seventy to eighty yards from the bait. This still results in a good, close shot—and allows at least a little movement during the wait.

Though distance is no problem when hunting bear over a bait, a primary challenge is that bear, especially bigger bear, almost always come at last light. To complicate the problem, a good bait is set close to heavy cover so the bear will feel secure in its approach. The hunter must take a black animal in black shadow—and he must take it cleanly, because nobody wants to stumble around in dark woods looking for a wounded bear!

Hunters take a lot of bear through chance encounter, by wandering around in the woods looking for something else while bear season is open and there's a tag in the pocket. Under such conditions the shots can vary infinitely, from a close encounter to a shot at considerable range. The same is true of spot-and-stalk bear hunting, but the technique is different. Spot-and-stalk, or glassing, is a common bear-hunting technique in the western United States, Canada, and Alaska. For this method the terrain must have scattered openings where bear might be moving and feeding—and you also need enough relief so you can gain vantage points and see some of these likely spots. Then you need a bear population that is dense enough so that you aren't looking for a needle in a haystack. When conditions meet these criteria, and when you use good optics intelligently, it's amazing how many bear you can see.

Feeding areas are key to spotting bear. In spring, bear come out to feed on new grass, so hunters glass bear slides, sedge-grass beaches, and recent clear-cuts in logged areas. Winter-killed carcasses are also an obvious draw. In fall, berry patches are prime places to glass. Sometimes you'll look all day and never see a bear, and sometimes you'll see a half-dozen. On a hunt on Vancouver Island, guide Guy Shockey, Kevin Howard, and I once glassed twenty-six bear in a single day, a truly incredible number. Bear are actually easy to spot and are visible at great distances. At first you glass every burnt stump, but after you've seen a bear, you recognize the difference: Even a brown black bear is darker and shinier than any stump!

The Perfect Shot: Mini Edition for North America II

The stalk concludes when you're close enough to make an absolutely certain fatal shot. Optimally, that means within a hundred yards, but sometimes wind or intervening terrain and vegetation won't allow it. I don't approve of genuinely long shots at any tough or potentially dangerous animal, but in spot-and-stalk hunting you should be armed and prepared for at least a two-hundred-yard shot, perhaps a bit more if you have the confidence, the skill, and the right equipment.

Taking the Shot

The average black bear is no heavier and probably not much tougher than the average white-tailed buck. Bear do have heavy shoulder and leg bones and incredibly solid musculature, but they are not bulletproof, and certainly the average two-hundred-pound bear is no tougher than a three-hundred-pound northern white-tailed buck. No matter the size, black bear can be dangerous. Even a small black bear can be incredibly fast and ferocious. The three men I know who were mauled by small black bear were literally torn from end to end. All spent some serious hospital time, and all have some interesting scars to show. I'm not sure they'd be alive to show them had they encountered a really big bear!

Making the perfect shot is always desirable, and it becomes particularly important when you encounter any animal that just might turn the tables if you mess up. Head shots are especially bad on bear and cat because only skull measurements are used. Though a brain shot will surely work, it will also ruin an interesting trophy and, if the bear is big enough, will preclude entry into the record books. Even if you don't care about that, the head shot is just too dicey because the target is very small, and shot placement must be absolutely perfect. Neck and spine shots are just as tricky. Bear have thick necks and broad backs, and it isn't easy to visualize exactly where the spine lies. It's far better to forget the fancy stuff and go for the surest shot. In this regard bear are the same as all other game: Heart shots and well-placed lung shots are absolutely fatal.

Both shots are just a wee bit tricky with bear. The lungs sit a bit farther forward, tucked in a bit closer behind the shoulder than is the case with ungulates. The heart sits very low, perfectly guarded by the massive shoulders. The lung shot is much the same as with other game: On a broadside presentation, follow the rear line of the foreleg one-third of the way up the body. The difference is that you don't have much leeway. With antlered game, a shot just a couple inches too far back will still be immediately fatal, but on bear you'll be just on the edge.

The shoulder/heart shot is also similar to that used on most other game: Follow the centerline of the foreleg into the center of the first third of the body. I prefer this shot, but not because it's easier; it really isn't. You've got plenty of leeway if you're a bit high or a couple of inches too far back, because you'll be well into the lungs—but if you're low, all you'll do is break a leg, and if you're a bit forward, you'll get brisket and, probably, a lost bear. However, the shoulder/heart shot is particularly good because bear show very little reaction to "bullet shock." A bear might drop to a shot that isn't immediately fatal, but it won't stay down very long. To get a bear down on the spot you need to hit it hard, preferably breaking heavy bone as well as wrecking the heart and lungs.

The Perfect Shot: Mini Edition for North America II

Obviously, you need a broadside presentation and a heavy bullet to get both shoulders. If at all possible, that's what you should wait for. Quartering shots that take either the on or off shoulder as well as the heart and/or lungs are almost as good, but I really don't like facing shots on bears, and I won't take a going-away shot on an unwounded bear.

The Right Bear

Bear go into the record books based on skull measurements, but skull size is almost impossible to judge. It's better to concentrate on body size on the generally correct theory that a big bear will have a big skull. Even this is hard to judge, and it takes a lot of experience. On a bait you can judge body size by reference points, but in most situations you must look for subtle indicators. A big bear swaggers or waddles as it walks, with feet that seem to be wide apart. The ears appear small and set well apart on the skull. With bear, the adage that "the big ones look big" generally holds true.

With black bear any bear that "squares" six feet is a nice bear, anywhere. (Lay out the hide with no stretching, measure across the front paws, then measure from nose to tail. Divide by two for the "square of the bear.") There are some areas where "seven-foot bear" are relatively common, and you may encounter eight-footers. However, there are two other considerations, and, depending on how you feel about it, they may be even more important than size. First and foremost is a well-furred hide. Always look for rubbed spots and avoid bears that have them; look for a bear that has a thick, silky, uniform hide. Then there's color. In areas that have bear of different color phases, you can hunt for color or you can hunt for size—but you can't always find both in the same bear.

Guns and Loads

You can take black bear effectively with any good deer cartridge from .270 upward. The various .30-calibers from .308 Winchester on up are excellent choices. However, there's a difference between just killing a bear and stopping it—not necessarily in a charge, but before it gets into heavy cover and you have to go dig it out.

I have taken a lot of bear with .270s, 7mms, and .30-calibers, and I've never had any serious problems—but with one of these I've never had a bear go down in its tracks and stay there. I like cartridges that aren't necessarily more powerful, in terms of energy, but that carry heavier bullets of larger caliber. Exactly what you choose depends on how you hunt. For hound hunting you need a light, fast, easy-to-carry rifle that will produce a lot of punch at nearly point-blank range. A .44 Magnum in either a carbine or a handgun, firing heavy-for-caliber bullets (for instance, 300-grain bullets rather than the standard pistol bullets) works well. So do old-timers like the .35 Remington. In North America, hound hunting is one of the few types of hunting where open sights are superior to scopes. If the bear bays on the ground or gets out of the tree, you must take your shot at very close range and be cognizant of the dogs darting in and out while you're doing it.

The Perfect Shot: Mini Edition for North America II

In bait hunting you certainly don't need a flat-shooting rifle, but you do need a low-powered scope that will gather lots of light. This is the ideal place for a "brush cartridge" like a .356 or .358 Winchester, a .375 Winchester, a .444 Marlin, or a good old .45-70.

With spot-and-stalk hunting you probably shouldn't consider a shot much past 250 yards on any bear, but you do need a bit of reach because you can't always get close to bear. The perfect cartridges for stalking black bear are the faster .35s—the old .350 Remington Magnum and the .35 Whelen. A .30-06 will do the job, as always—but I don't believe there's such a thing as too much gun for bear. Far better are the .33-calibers, the .338 Winchester Magnum, and all the rest. For the record, I have taken many black bear with a .375 H&H, and I have never, ever felt overgunned.

For this kind of hunting you should have a scoped rifle, but you don't need a whole lot of magnification, and you should be prepared for a very close shot as well as a longer shot. A scope in the 1.75–5X range is adequate, but the newer 1.75–6X scopes or a 2–7X are probably ideal.

Bullet Performance
With bear this should be an easy decision. You want tough, heavy-for-caliber bullets. Period. The only black bear I have ever seen lost was shot squarely on the shoulder—perfect shot placement—with a 150-grain .270. The loss occurred because the bullet, although heavy-for-caliber, was a quick-opening conventional softpoint, and it just didn't penetrate. With bear you

want bullets in the medium-for-caliber or, better, heavy-for-caliber range: 180- to 200-grain in .30-caliber; 225- to 250-grain in .33-caliber; 250-grain in .35-caliber. And you want them to be of strong design, like Nosler Partition, Swift A-Frame, Winchester Fail Safe, Trophy Bonded Bear Claw, and Barnes X-Bullet. Shot placement is always critical, but with bear you must also penetrate those heavy bones and corded muscles.

Grizzly & Alaskan Brown Bear

To anchor a bear, smash the shoulder bone with a good bullet. A brain shot is not recommended unless the bear is charging and must be stopped on the spot. Shown here is the triad of heart, lung, and shoulder shots. (Photo courtesy of Len Rue Jr.)

GRIZZLY & ALASKAN BROWN BEAR
Hunting the humpbacked is deadly serious business!

The grizzly bear and the Alaskan brown bear are really the same species, now designated *Ursus arctos*. Lewis and Clark found plenty of bears on the Great Plains, and most of California was superb grizzly country. But men and grizzly didn't agree, and during the nineteenth century the grizzly was either eradicated or pushed into the remotest areas. Today, there is no such thing as a plains grizzly or a California grizzly—but thank God there are still grizzly, and they are even staging a slight comeback.

There have always been remnant grizzly in Montana's remotest country. Today the populations in both Yellowstone National Park and Glacier National Park are spilling over, so grizzly sightings are relatively common throughout the region. The occasional wanderer turns up in Washington, and a grizzly was killed in an encounter with a man in Colorado some years ago. It is still rumored—but not confirmed—that a small population of Mexican grizzly may be hanging on in central Chihuahua's Sierra del Nido. But the Yellowstone-Glacier ecosystem represents the only viable grizzly population left in the continental United States, and currently there is no hunting for this bear type.

This is sad. Though relatively few of us will ever hunt grizzly bear, such a hunt must surely be the dream of most American hunters. To take the "horrible bear" in fair chase truly is an ultimate sporting experience, and little opportunity remains. Today, despite the many

Even with premium bullets, a brown/grizzly bear can be shot only when at a 90-degree angle. Almost all guides advise the hunter to keep shooting till the animal no longer moves. Good advice! (Photo courtesy of Len Rue Jr.)

identified (and often hotly disputed) races and subspecies, we know that the Alaskan brown bear and the grizzly bear are the same animal. However, it is also absolutely proper for us hunters to consider them differently, not only in our record books but also in our hunting plans and dreams.

The grizzly bear is an interior bear, the bear of the high mountains and timbered valleys. Today it remains fairly plentiful from the Alberta Rockies west through British Columbia, and from western Northwest Territories west through interior Alaska. Hunting opportunities are shrinking; it is now protected in Alberta, and, somewhat inexplicably, it is not hunted in the Mackenzie district of Northwest Territories, although this area holds good numbers of this bear. Even British Columbia, with a large and healthy population, was briefly closed in 2000–2001 due to political pressure from antihunters. At this writing the grizzly is hunted in British Columbia, Yukon, the barrens of Northwest Territories, and Alaska. Although in total there are plenty of grizzly, hunting them is extremely difficult because they are widely scattered across big and rugged country. A grizzly hunt is a lengthy and difficult quest.

The size of a grizzly depends largely on climate and available food, but genetics also play a role. As with black bear, almost any area can produce a huge bear—but in the northern mountains most grizzly are not that large. The record books only record skull measurements for bears. Skull size, however, is almost impossible to judge, but it is the only irrefutable, unchangeable measure of a bear's size. One might assume that eight-foot grizzly are normal. This is not the case. Especially in the harsh climate of the interior mountains, a grizzly that

The Perfect Shot: Mini Edition for North America II

squares 6½ to 7 feet and weighs 350 to 400 pounds is a pretty good bear. Eight-foot grizzly, and occasionally the genuine nine-footer, do occur. But they are rare, and they are most likely found where climatic conditions allow a longer growing season and where the diet is especially good. British Columbia's Bella Coola region is famous for big grizzly—and these are fish-fed bear. Alaska's Seward Peninsula, although very far north, also has salmon streams and plentiful moose, and the bear grow big. Just a short distance farther north and east, in the Brooks Range, the bear are beautifully furred but rarely large.

This illustrates the real difference between Alaskan brown bear and inland grizzly. They are really the same bear, but Alaska's southeast coast, Kenai Peninsula, Alaskan Peninsula, and her southern islands are warmed by Japanese currents and cut with salmon streams. The bear eat better and hibernate for shorter periods—and they grow much larger. The line between the two is man-made and indistinct, and the bear care little about it. On the boundary a bear might be a very large grizzly one day and a medium-sized Alaskan brown bear the next. Generally, the Alaskan brown bear is considerably larger than the grizzly. At its best it is huge.

Everyone talks about the ten-foot brown bear. It exists, but brown bear that actually reach these dimensions (without stretching the hide before measuring) are very rare. An eight-foot brown bear is a good trophy, and such a bear will probably weigh seven hundred pounds. A genuine nine-foot bear is a very good trophy, and might weigh as much as half a ton. The ten-footers, for those who are fortunate to find them, are genuine monsters, with weights that might exceed fifteen hundred pounds. Brown bear hunting is, on average, more successful than grizzly hunting because brown bear congregate by the salmon streams.

Shots at the Big Bear

Whether you're hunting grizzly or Alaskan brown bear, you'll almost certainly hunt them by spot-and-stalk techniques. The only alternatives are tracking if there's snow, or still-hunting along a salmon stream. Because of the mountainous country in which they live, shots at grizzly probably average a bit longer; close encounters are more common in the alder thickets of good brown bear country.

Either way, shots can vary from extremely close to not much more than two hundred yards. You can see bear from much greater distances—the humpbacked bear are huge animals, and it isn't uncommon to glass them at distances of several miles. But you usually won't shoot them where you first see them. The game is stalking, not necessarily to get as close as you can but to get close enough that your shot is absolutely sure. This should be the goal with all game, but it means something different with an animal as large, tough, and potentially dangerous as a big bear. With a good centerfire rifle, the goal should be to keep your shots within a hundred yards or so, and if you do it right you should be able to get that close—sometimes.

The big bear aren't gifted with particularly good eyesight. If you move slowly and quietly, keeping off the skyline and using a bit of cover, you can usually get close enough for a good

Once a hunter decides to hunt a grizzly, he needs to start thinking about larger calibers and heavier, well-constructed bullets. (Photo courtesy of Dušan Smetana) shot—if the wind holds. Bear have an extremely keen sense of smell, and this forms their first line of defense, as well as their primary means of locating food. Never underestimate the power of a bear's nose!

Even if the wind holds perfectly, it isn't always possible to get as close as you would like. There are many other reasons for this. The bear might be moving into heavy cover, or it might be in cover so thick that you can see it from where you are but wouldn't be able to see it from over there.

Taking the Shot

Grizzly bear are incredibly powerful creatures. They live long, hard lives in tough country, and I have watched them excavate Volkswagen-size boulders in search of a bite-sized marmot. They are not much impressed by bullet energy. They must be hit very hard in the right place. Even then, the clean, one-shot kills we all prefer are unusual. They absolutely will not happen unless you place that first shot almost perfectly.

You should generally avoid brain and spine shots, primarily because they're just too tricky. There's almost no margin for error, and if there is error, the only possible results are a lost bear or a dangerous encounter with a wounded animal. Also, since bear enter the record books based on skull measurements, a head shot will ruin an important trophy. As on all game, the lung-shot bear is deadly, but on big bear you need to add the modifier "eventually." A lung-shot grizzly can cover a lot of ground. If you have stalked it well, it probably won't know where you are when the shot goes off, but it might well come your way. It's far better to break heavy bone, shooting through the heavy shoulder bone into the heart.

A bear's heart is very low in the chest and almost perfectly centered between the forelegs. On a broadside presentation, follow the centerline of the foreleg a bit less than a third of the way up. This is the shoulder/heart shot, by far the best option for a really big bear. You can't always get the perfect presentation, and this presents a dilemma. On these animals you need a really good shot angle, or you don't have a shot at all. On the other hand, the hunts are very expensive, and there aren't many opportunities. Waiting for that perfect broadside presentation isn't always the wisest course.

Just remember that you simply must get your bullet into the heart/lung area. Angled shots will work if the angle isn't too steep and you have plenty of gun and bullet—but you must be able to visualize exactly where the vitals lie and adjust your aim accordingly.

The Right Bear

Sometimes a decent-size brown or grizzly bear can be almost impossible to find, and sometimes it's easy. There isn't much you can do about this, other than to try hard to put yourself in a good area and then hunt hard when you get there. In the better areas most coastal brown bear hunts will be successful, but even in the best areas few grizzly hunts offer more than 50 percent success rate. Supposing you do spot a bear, the next challenges are figuring out how big it is and then deciding if it meets your expectations. Neither is simple.

Grizzly & Alaskan Brown Bear

Bear are extremely hard to judge. If you're working from tracks, you will have a pretty good idea of the size of the bear, but judging a bear on a distant hillside is difficult. On my first brown bear hunt, my guide, Slim Gale, told me to look for a bear with a small head. This sounded odd, because it takes a huge skull to make the record book. He told me: "They've all got big heads, so if the head looks small, the body is huge."

Maybe. One morning, from more than a mile away, Slim got a quick glance at a bear and said that we had to go after it. It was early in the hunt, so I wasn't sure. Slim was sure. "Man, that's a ten-foot bear. Let's go!"

The bear measured eleven feet, two inches, across the front paws and ten feet, eight inches, nose to tail—a giant of a bear. But how did Slim know? Simply because he has seen a lot of bear. Other indicators of size are a swaying, swaggering walk and ears that look tiny and set far apart on a huge skull. It isn't easy to be sure, unless your guide is experienced.

Another problem is unreasonable expectations. This problem is far more severe with Alaskan brown bear than it is with grizzly bear. Most hunters accept that grizzly are extremely hard to come by. A huge bear would be nice, but any well-furred, mature grizzly taken in fair chase is a great trophy—especially after a week or ten days of extremely hard hunting. Brown bear are different, and it's partly the fault of people like me, whose writings seem to suggest that ten-foot bear grow on trees. Everybody wants a ten-foot bear, but very few people will ever see one. They exist, and sometimes they seem to come out of the woodwork. In the best Peninsula or Kodiak areas, an outfitter might take two or three such bear in a single season and then not see another for a couple of years.

The Perfect Shot: Mini Edition for North America II

The sad part is that, armed with unrealistic expectations, too many hunters turn down perfectly good trophy bear in the search for a monster. Then they either go home empty-handed or, in the closing days, take a bear smaller than others they have passed up. The average bear taken on the Peninsula and on Kodiak Island, by both residents and nonresidents, is less than eight feet. So, unless you're prepared to return year after year, a well-furred, eight-foot bear (honestly measured) is a good brown bear and a fine trophy.

Guns and Loads

I am a firm believer in powerful rifles firing heavy-for-caliber, well-constructed bullets. Make no mistake: You can take any bear that walks—especially the smaller grizzly—with a .270, 7mm, or .30 caliber loaded with a good bullet. Many brown bear are taken every year with popular deer cartridges like these, but that's not the issue. The smaller calibers will surely kill big bear, but only if both shot presentation and shot placement are perfect. This severely limits the shot angles that you can practically take, which means that you may not be able to take advantage of the only opportunity you get. Perhaps more important, the smaller calibers may not have enough steam to get you out of trouble if something goes wrong. Shot placement isn't always perfect, so it's important to be able to stop the bear, which is different from just killing it.

The classic broadside presentation is always the most desirable, but you might not get that opportunity. There are plenty of other options if you have enough gun and enough bullet to do the job. I shot a bear in the Skeenas that was feeding on a slanting hogback, head downhill, facing directly toward us. I waited a little while, but the light was going and the presentation didn't change. My position was steady and I had plenty of gun, although at 250 yards the range was long. I was shooting a .340 Weatherby Magnum with a 250-grain Nosler Partition, and I had plenty of confidence in that gun and that load. So I put the cross hairs right behind the head and just in front of the hump, expecting the big bullet to break the spine and penetrate down into the chest cavity. It did more than that, exiting between the bear's front legs, but I doubt the bear was aware of that. It was already dead.

Grizzly bear are smaller than brown bear, and they may also be taken at somewhat greater range because of their mountainous habitat. You could get by just fine with a .300 magnum firing heavy bullets, and the .375s (.375 H&H, .375 Remington Ultra Mag, .375 Weatherby Magnum, and so on) pose no handicap. But I believe the 8mm Remington Magnum and the fast .33s, from .338 Winchester Magnum upward, are just perfect.

These cartridges also work well on brown bear. A few years ago I shot a very big Siberian brown bear, essentially identical to the Alaskan variety, with the same .340 Weatherby Magnum. The bear was striding toward me through deep snow, and at sixty yards it paused and quartered slightly to me. I put the cross hairs just inside the on-shoulder. This is a tough shot because with any frontal presentation you have to be just right or you'll catch just one lung or, worse, skin just inside the shoulder, and you'll do little damage. This time I got it right. The bullet centered the heart, then penetrated through the rest of the bear, coming to rest against the hide on the far hip.

The Perfect Shot: Mini Edition for North America II

The bear's reaction was a tribute to this animal's stamina. It was clearly dead, but it showed no reaction other than to charge to the right in a cloud of snow, disappearing behind some trees. It was dead when I reached it a few seconds later—but even a cartridge as powerful as the .340 didn't stop it! I bow to the consensus of Alaska's professional brown-bear guides, who, on average, reckon the good old .375 H&H is the best of all brown bear cartridges.

Mind you, many guides carry .338s, which will certainly do the job. Others carry open-sighted big-bores; a smattering of big-lever actions in .450 Marlin or .45-70 with hopped-up handloads; a lot of .458s; and even the occasional double-barrel Nitro Express. But the brown bear guide's primary concern is stopping an enraged bear if the need arises.

As hunters, our primary concern is killing it with a perfect shot. For our purpose we want a rifle topped with a low-powered scope, chambered to a cartridge that will cleanly take the biggest of bear, not only in a close encounter but also at two hundred yards if necessary. The .375s—the old H&H as well as the faster .375s, like the .375 Remington Ultra Mag and .375 Weatherby Magnum—are easily the best choices.

Bullet Performance

Penetration, penetration, penetration. Big bears are massive creatures with dense muscles and extremely heavy bones. No matter what cartridge you choose, you must mate it with tough, well-constructed, heavy-for-caliber bullets designed to penetrate. Note that the lighter the caliber, the more important it is to use the toughest, deepest-penetrating bullets available—but

Grizzly & Alaskan Brown Bear

28

even with big cartridges like the .375 you want tough bullets. A really big brown bear is every bit as big as an African Cape buffalo and asks just as much of a bullet to ensure penetration.

When I shot that monster Alaskan brown bear in 1981, I was carrying a .375 H&H, but I had it loaded with then-new 300-grain Sierra boattails. That's plenty of gun and plenty of bullet weight, but those early .375-caliber Sierras had thinner jackets than these bullets do today, and their penetrating qualities weren't up to task. I shot the bear five times, all good hits, finally managing to stop it just short of some dense alders that I did not wish to enter. In part this happened because it was a grand old bear, big and tough and unwilling to give up. But I will always believe that, with the shot placement I had, tougher bullets like the Nosler Partition, Trophy Bonded Bear Claw, Barnes X-Bullet, Swift A-Frame, or Winchester Fail Safe would have done better. Note that, of these great, tough, penetrating bullets, only the Nosler Partition was available back then. Today we have a great choice of fine bullets, ideally suited to almost every occasion. There really is no excuse not to tailor the bullet to the game at hand, and, with the biggest bear, you want the toughest bullets available.

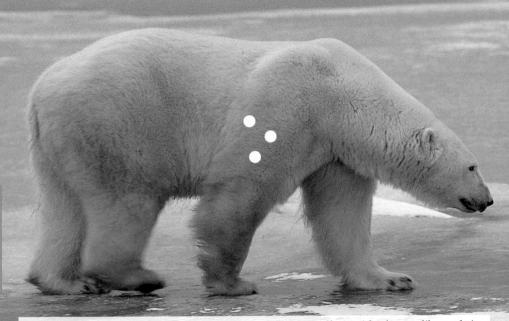

Polar Bear

A polar bear hunt will likely be a once-in-a-lifetime adventure. Shoot with a large caliber and aim, if possible, to break the shoulder bone, which is the most forward shot indicated. (Photo courtesy of Leonard Lee Rue III)

POLAR BEAR
Man is just another meal!

The polar bear, *Ursus maritimus*, which grows to incredible size on its diet of seals and anything else it can find, ranks as the most dangerous game in North America. Why? First, the polar bear has never learned to fear man. Although the Inuit have hunted polar bear along the fringes of their range for centuries, pressure from sport hunters has always been light and on the edges of the polar bear's vast, frigid domain. Most polar bear live and die without ever encountering a human being. When they find one of the strange two-legged creatures, they regard it as nothing more than another morsel of animal protein in their never-ending search for food. Upon scenting man, most black, brown, and grizzly bears will head the other way. The polar bear may run, but it's just as likely to rub its tummy and come on in for supper. The second reason the polar bear is so dangerous has to do with its environment. As dangerous as the polar bear is, the weather and the cold it thrives in are even more dangerous. Temperatures of fifty and sixty degrees below zero are common, and deadly storms can come out of nowhere. Polar bear habitat is not man's habitat, and in that icy world a slight mishap can mean death.

Hunting polar bear by dogsled out on the pack ice is the most difficult and challenging hunt available to sportsmen anywhere in the world, and certainly one of the most dangerous. A limited amount of ground—*er*, ice—can be covered by dogsled, so the hunts take a lot

Many people have heard how the Inuit of the North shoot polar bears with very small calibers; however, this is not advisable for the sport hunter. Note how the position of the heart is quite far back when the animal is taking long strides, as shown in this picture. (Photo courtesy of Leonard Lee Rue III)

of time. Most hunters are actually out on the ice two to three weeks. This extreme cold is dangerous in itself, especially for those of us who hail from warmer climates. The Inuit guides work hard to take care of their hunters, but they can't always keep us from making mistakes, and mistakes can be costly. Frostbite is common, usually caused by forgetting to change socks, taking off a glove in the excitement of shooting a bear, or stoically (and foolishly) keeping your mouth shut and ignoring a problem when you realize there's one.

The polar bear truly is a marine mammal, and most polar bear, especially the big boars, never touch dry land throughout their lives. Many do come ashore on the Arctic Islands, and in North America a lot of bear, primarily sows with cubs, come down onto the mainland. Churchill on Hudson Bay is famous for its polar bear. Polar bear are confined to the northern polar ice cap, but it is not exclusively a North American animal. They are found in the waters off Greenland, Iceland, and Norway; they are also found above Siberia's northern coastline. It is said that the Russian polar bear are among the largest.

Shots at White Bear

These days polar-bear hunts by dogsled are largely a matter of simply covering ground until you either spot a bear or find fresh tracks. Nothing on earth is as open as the pack ice, so there is obvious potential for long shooting. When the Inuit spot a bear, they typically close the distance until the bear becomes alarmed, then set free some of the sled dogs, and a spot-and-stalk hunt instantly becomes similar to a hound hunt for black bear. If everything goes right, the dogs distract the bear until the hunters can approach within range. There are exceptions to this scenario, however.

On the open ice a bear can simply outdistance its pursuers, and there also may be escape routes. The Canadian ice doesn't have as many open leads, but they do occur, and only bear and the other marine mammals can swim in the icy water found there. There are also pressure ridges, huge and jagged uplifts created by the constant shifting of the great plates of ice. Bear can negotiate them; dogsleds cannot. So there are times when a longer shot may be required to prevent a bear from going where humans cannot follow.

Then there are the occasional surprises. A polar bear will usually flee when caught on the open ice. This is a natural reaction—but this doesn't mean it is afraid. During the long Arctic nights, when the camp is quiet, the polar bear is just as likely to come calling, enticed by the aromas of food cooking, tasty sled dogs, and morsels of strange-looking creatures on two legs. During the hunt, you may search the endless ice for days and weeks looking for sign of a bear—but the bear you're looking for is just as likely to come into camp looking for you. A significant number of polar-bear hunts end when the bear wanders into camp and the sled dogs go crazy—which means that a very close shot is every bit as likely as a long one!

Taking the Shot

With an animal as big, powerful, and potentially dangerous as a polar bear, the choice for a perfect shot should be obvious. The best option is to shoot for heavy bone, aiming to break one or both shoulders while penetrating the chest cavity and taking out the heart and lungs. With a broadside presentation, simply follow the centerline of the foreleg no more than one-third up the body. You need a tough bullet, preferably heavy-for-caliber, to break the shoulder bone and penetrate the heart—but a well-constructed bullet of appropriate caliber will do this, and if you have enough power the bullet will keep going and will smash the opposite shoulder as well. This is the kind of performance you want. On shots with less optimum presentation, you probably have no chance to take out both shoulders, but you must visualize where the heart lies—low and well protected between the shoulders—and direct your bullet accordingly. A standard lung shot will surely kill the bear, but in my experience the big bear are so tough that they can withstand even a perfect lung shot long enough to cause dangerous mayhem. On this type of animal I am convinced that a shoulder/heart shot is the best approach.

The Right Bear

Although polar bear enter the record book based on skull measurements, almost no one can accurately judge skull size. Look for the biggest bear you can find, though even this is complicated by the featureless Arctic terrain. Tracks are the most reliable indicator; a big track almost always indicates a big bear. A trophy bear should be a mature specimen, preferably a boar but certainly a lone traveler. Today an eight-foot bear you have taken by dogsled, not only in fair chase but on one of the world's most arduous hunts, is a great trophy. Nine-foot, ten-foot, and even larger bear are out there, but if you pass up an average specimen, there is a very good chance that you have just walked away from your polar bear.

Guns and Loads

Throughout this book I will make few references to action type. In many cases the cartridge will dictate the action you choose, but most of the time it really doesn't matter whether you choose a lever action, slide action, semiauto, or single-shot, provided you are comfortable with your choice. In this case it does matter. Because of the potential danger and because it can be extremely difficult to fumble for cartridges in the extreme cold, you need a repeating rifle when hunting polar bear. You also need a rifle that will be absolutely reliable in the subzero cold. To me this means a bolt action because the bolt action is the easiest action to degrease, and it will work best with just a bit of dry graphite lubricant. Before embarking on a polar-bear hunt, strip the bolt completely and soak all the parts in a good degreasing agent. Then reassemble with just a touch of dry graphite lubricant. A low-powered scope is absolutely necessary, but the polar-bear rifle should also have detachable mounts and auxiliary iron sights that are properly zeroed. This is essential because equipment takes a tremendous pounding on the dogsled day after day.

The proper cartridge takes a bit of thought. The Inuit shoot polar bear with the rifles they have. Historically, the local hunters—not only highly skilled but incredibly brave—used what they had. Spears eventually gave way to .30-30 Winchesters and .303 Enfields. Then the accurate little .222 became extremely popular. It is ideal for hunting seal, an Inuit staple, and was widely used for polar bear as well. Privately, however, Inuit hunters have admitted that they usually had to shoot their bear a number of times. Today the 7mm Remington Magnum is extremely common in the Inuit communities.

Personally, I believe these cartridges are not a good choice. The possibility of needing to anchor a bear at longer range suggests that a fast .33, like a .340 Weatherby or .338 Remington Ultra Mag, would be good. That is true, and with a well-constructed 250-grain bullet it would also stop a charge at close range. However, I know the good old .375 is better medicine for Alaskan brown bear than the .33s. Polar bear are of similar size, but the wide-open ice and the possibility of a longer shot complicate the situation. For the ultimate polar-bear cartridges, I would look to the faster .375s: the .375 Remington Ultra Mag, .375 Weatherby Magnum, and .378 Weatherby Magnum. These offer the large-caliber and heavy-bullet punch of a .375, but flatten the trajectory considerably more than what the old .375 H&H can offer.

Bullet Performance

Bullets must be heavy-for-caliber and tough. Even with a perfect broadside presentation, the bullet must get through a lot of bear—dense muscle, heavy bone, resilient hide. Shooting a fairly stout cartridge helps, but bullet performance is even more important than choice of cartridge. On this hunt you want the toughest, deepest-penetrating bullets made! Depending on your cartridge and choice of ammo, think about Barnes X-Bullet, Swift A-Frame, Winchester Fail Safe, and Nosler Partition.

Many bison get shot in the brain spine to ensure an instantaneo kill; however, these shots require ve accurate shot placement. (Pho courtesy of Leonard Lee Rue III)

BISON
Beware of the hair!

The American bison, *Bison bison*, is one of the world's largest bovines. It is larger than a Cape buffalo and larger than an Asian water buffalo. Anyone who has been around bison, wild or domesticated, knows they are not barnyard cattle. They are almost impossible to fence, they are unpredictable as hell, and they can be downright dangerous. We should not underestimate the bison, for any bovine weighing more than a ton is a formidable creature!

Ancestors of the American bison crossed the land bridge from Siberia thousands of years ago. At one time their range extended across Alaska, down the Rocky Mountain chain into Mexico, and east to the Appalachians. Here in North America two subspecies are generally recognized: the plains bison (*Bison bison bison*) and the woodland bison (*Bison bison athabascae*). The plains bison existed from the Rocky Mountains eastward, and the woodland bison extended from the western slopes of the Rockies north to the Northwest Territories and to the west across Alaska. The woodland bison is larger and darker, but the only pure specimens are found in sanctuaries in the Northwest Territories and Alberta.

The American bison is a very large, woolly coated animal, with mature bulls averaging over a ton and occasionally weighing as much as three thousand pounds. The horns are short and very thick, curving out and up from the sides of the skull. During the hot plains summers, the bison appear almost mangy, but their winter coats become thick and

Bison

A bison, often erroneously called a "buffalo," is easily North America's largest land mammal. Mature bull biso[n] weigh more than Cape buffalo. If body shots are taken, anything considered for a Cape buffalo should be though[t] of for the bison. A sensible minimum would be a .375. (Photo courtesy of Leonard Lee Rue III) luxurious. In cold climates, they grow a long skullcap of woolly hair that obscures the base of the horns.

Bison are fairly prolific, so there are plenty of opportunities to shoot them—but there is little opportunity to actually hunt one. With very few exceptions, modern bison hunting is purely herd management, carried out under controlled conditions. The opportunity to hunt free-range bison by genuine fair chase probably exists only in the Henry Mountains herd in Utah and a couple of free-range herds in Alaska. In most situations, taking a bison is more of a collection than a hunt. This is neither bad nor good; it just is.

Shots at Bison

Bison are an open-country, grazing animal. They are not naturally wary, and today's herds are so carefully managed that flight at long range is unlikely. There are always reasons why you can't get particularly close to any game—such as wind direction and natural obstacles—but it is unlikely that you will make a long-range shot at bison, and I certainly would not recommend it on such a large beast. Most of the time you can close within a hundred yards with relative ease, and then it's just a matter of placing the shot.

Taking the Shot

Legend has it that the old-time buffalo hunters stood off several hundred yards with their big Sharps rifles and dropped bison after bison in their tracks. With the arcing trajectories of the black-powder rifles, "long range" was a relative figure. The idea was to stand off far enough so that the smoke and belch of the rifle didn't disturb the bison but close enough for every valuable cartridge to count. A hundred yards was too close, but two hundred yards was a long shot. The rifles were accurate, and the hunters were extremely skilled, but this was business. They didn't try head shots, and they avoided shoulder/heart shots because the animal was certain to make a death run and spook the rest of the herd. Instead, they concentrated on lung shots.

Unless rutting or angered, the bison is a phlegmatic beast, not subject to bullet shock. It usually takes a bullet through the lungs quite calmly, continues to feed for a while, and then lies down and eventually dies. The old buffalo hunters concentrated on this shot: safe, sure, and least likely to cause a stampede. We modern hunters want to take our game more quickly and cleanly, so this is not the shot we want.

Under many circumstances today, the bison hunter gets the skin and trophy, but the meat goes to the market—so hunters insist on head and neck shots. The neck shot is difficult with bison. The neck is extremely deep, and within the neck the spine dips very far down as it enters the region of the body. It's hard to visualize shot placement and altogether too easy to get it wrong. The brain shot is never easy, but it's a bit easier to visualize. On a broadside presentation, shoot just under the horn and your bison should drop to the shot. From the front it's much trickier, but you must shoot for the center of the skull just under the horns.

Bison

If body shots are appropriate, they are by far the safest course. A shoulder/heart shot is the best approach, but only if you're shooting a powerful rifle with tough bullets that will penetrate. Just follow the centerline of the foreleg up into the bottom third of the body, and you will have your bison. Unless you're shooting an elephant gun, it probably won't go down instantly, but it will go down.

The Right Bull

A really huge bison will have horn length in the upper teens. Horn mass comes with age, and it's the mass and how that mass is carried throughout the horns that really makes the trophy. This is not easy to judge, but beware of horns that appear sharp and thin, regardless of length. It's best to shoot bison during the winter; the luxurious coat is every bit as important to trophy quality as the horns. The long hair on the head makes judging trophies even more difficult. Often you cannot see the bases at all, and the hair comes up as high as the horns. This in itself is a tip-off: If a winter bull has horns that extend above the hairline, take a good look at the mass. The curve is also important; you get a lot more length along a curved horn than you do from a straight horn.

Guns and Loads

Because of the relatively open country and the controlled circumstances under which bison are hunted today, you could certainly use a .30-06 with a good, tough bullet and be

The Perfect Shot: Mini Edition for North America II

perfectly safe—especially if you take a brain shot. I used my old Winchester Model 71 in .348 for a South Dakota bison, and it would have been just perfect if I had made the brain shot correctly. But I didn't. It took several body shots to correct the error, and that is the common result if you don't have enough gun. You wouldn't think of taking on a Cape buffalo with a .30-06 or a .348 Winchester, and bison are considerably larger. I think this huge animal deserves more respect.

Among modern rifles, think about the same cartridges you might use on African buffalo—the .375s and .416s. If you take a brain shot and do it right, the cartridge you're shooting probably won't matter much—but if you blow it, or you decide on a shoulder/heart shot because of distance or presentation, the big guns will deliver much more satisfactory performance.

Buffalo hunting today has a lot to do with nostalgia, so many hunters opt to use the old black-powder cartridges. The .45-70 is the most popular and most available of the old cartridges, but you must keep in mind that it's no powerhouse. Remember that the old-timers weren't nearly as concerned about clean kills as we are today. Using older cartridges certainly adds a different dimension to the hunt, but if you use one with traditional open sights, you have probably eliminated your ability to make a brain shot unless you are very close, and you aren't long on power for so large an animal.

Use heavy bullets, and, if you don't mind cheating, use modern heavy loads as well! A .45-70 in a strong, modern action loaded with good handloads becomes an altogether different cartridge, and it is far more adequate than the black-powder loads our forefathers used. In

December 2001, I used a single-shot Harrington & Richardson .45-70 to take a huge bison bull with John Ray in southern Colorado. The particular loads I used were black-powder handloads behind a hard-cast bullet, pushed a good deal faster than the standard load. Performance was superb. Regardless of the high-energy figures obtained with smaller, faster calibers, there's much to be said for the hitting power of big, heavy bullets! While I used black-powder loads for nostalgic reasons, modern .45-70 loads like the Garrett's (for use only in modern rifles) offer a great deal more power than anything used in the nineteenth century!

Bullet Performance

Regardless of the cartridge you choose, you simply must use bullets that will absolutely guarantee penetration. You want tough bullets that are heavy-for-caliber and well constructed. Bullet construction does depend on velocity; at the speeds of which a .45-70 is capable, hard-alloy bullets will absolutely penetrate. If you use a modern rifle, however, you should use modern bullets like Swift A-Frame, Barnes X-Bullet, and Winchester Fail Safe—especially if you use calibers less powerful than the .375 H&H.

Note how far back behind the leg the point of aim is for the heart shot.
(Photo courtesy of Len Rue Jr.)

COUGAR

The mountain lion may be America's most elusive animal . . .

Variously called cougar, mountain lion, catamount, panther, and painter, our long-tailed tawny cat is just one animal, *Felis concolor*. The cougar is one of nature's most efficient predators. Almost always a solitary hunter, it is able to bring down creatures many times its size—elk and even moose—with little difficulty. Deer are its natural and preferred prey, however. An adult cougar averages one deer per week, year in and year out.

The cougar is so elusive and secretive that sightings are fairly rare even where the great cat is common. Individual cats wander great distances, so a chance encounter a vast distance from known populations may not indicate a resident or breeding population. But sightings in the East, Southeast, and upper Midwest are now so common that it seems almost certain that the cougar—without any protection from man, save closed seasons—is reestablishing itself over much of its former range.

The cougar is generally an extremely shy beast when it comes to man, which may seem odd for so efficient a predator. It is probably fortunate for both cougar and the humans who encounter them that, at least historically, the cougar has rarely been aggressive and has almost never figured out that the two-legged creatures that invade its domain might be easier prey than deer. If our mountain lion had the disposition of the smaller but much more aggressive leopard, there would be many more historical accounts of

Cougar

Like other large cats of the world, cougars tend to have their hearts rather far back in the rib cage. (Photo courtesy of Len Rue Jr.)

cougar attacks, and the cougar would undoubtedly have been persecuted mercilessly. Though humans have always had an innate fear of hunting cats, there were very few genuine, documented cases of cougar attacking or attempting to prey upon humans—until recently.

In California the cougar is now a "nongame species," meaning that it is altogether beyond the control of the California Fish and Game Department. Fortunately, no other western states have followed this model, but most of the western states have shortened mountain lion seasons and enacted license quotas. Oregon has retained a liberal season but has outlawed the use of dogs. For those who wish to hunt a cougar, all this is unfortunate because the opportunity is shrinking. For everyone who loves wildlife, this is serious stuff, because wildlife's only hope for survival is through man's management.

Shots at Cougar

Historically, and to this day, the only truly reliable way to hunt a cougar is with a well-trained pack of hounds. The most difficult part of the hunt is finding a fresh trail for the dogs to follow. Good houndsmen usually know their country and have a good idea where to look, but most of the time it takes several days of scouring rugged canyons before a hunter can locate the track of a mature cat. Then the chase is on, and houndsmen live for this time. Like all cats, the cougar is relatively short-winded, but it will lead the dogs over the roughest country around. The length of

The Perfect Shot: Mini Edition for North America II

the chase also depends on the exact age of the tracks, and this is usually impossible to determine.

The primary opportunities to hunt cougar are in the western Rocky Mountains and western Canada. In the southern areas such as Arizona and Nevada, hunting cougar is usually a matter of dry land trailing without snow. This is considered difficult, and certainly it's more difficult to find and evaluate tracks—but the dogs are used to this. In northern areas cougar are generally hunted in snow, where it is much easier to size and age tracks but not necessarily to follow the hounds.

No matter where you hunt, the real key is a serious houndsman with a pack of well-trained dogs. Even with the best outfitter and the best pack, it is always possible you won't find the fresh tracks of a big cat, but this is unusual. Cougar hunting is generally very successful, especially if you give it ten days in good country. Eventually you will find a big track; the dogs will jump the cat, and after a heart-pounding chase the cat will either tree or bay up in rocky outcroppings. The shot, when it comes, will usually be very close and anticlimactic; the actual hunt is the chase.

Taking the Shot

Hunting cougar is the houndsman's game. He has trained the dogs, and he derives the greatest pleasure in seeing them work. The hunter who accompanies the houndsman in search of a cougar rug is little more than an observer—until it is time to take the shot. When that moment comes, the shot will probably be simple, but it must be done right. A wounded cat can wreak havoc on valuable dogs.

Head shots are out because cats are thin-skinned and fragile, and a head shot will not only ruin the skull but may also ruin the trophy. The only genuine options are lung shots or heart shots. Either is effective; the choice depends somewhat on the angle and presentation that is available. You don't always have a lot of choices, for the cat may be partly hidden and protected by branches in a stout tree, or it may be backed up a rocky crevice. In any case, it is absolutely essential that you hold your fire until you are certain of a killing shot.

The actual placement differs not at all from placement for most other four-footed game. For the heart shot, shoot into the bottom third of the chest between the forelegs; for the lung shot, shoot into the bottom half of the center third of the chest along the rear line of the foreleg.

The Right Cat

Northern cats average a bit larger than cats from southern climes, but anywhere cougar are hunted, a male tom will average 150 pounds. Weights over 200 pounds are possible but rare. Females are considerably smaller, usually running around 100 to 110 pounds. In most areas females without young are perfectly legal game, but a trophy cougar is a tom, and any mature tom is a great trophy. It is almost impossible to judge skull size, so serious houndsmen look for a large track, a reliable indicator of a big-bodied male. A big cougar

Many guides and houndsmen prefer a hunter to use a blunt-nosed .30-30 for a cougar with good reason because this combination has a great propensity for transmitting shock and energy. The heart shot is indicated. (Photo courtesy of Len Rue Jr.)

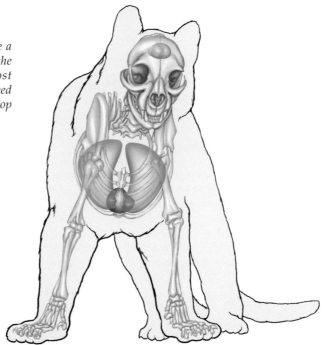

When a hunter is ready to take a shot, he will most likely find the cougar in this position. Most cougars are shot after being treed or confined to a high rocky outcrop by dogs.

will probably have a large skull, but it will certainly have a tawny hide that stretches eight feet or more from nose to tail—which is the real trophy of a cougar hunt.

Guns and Loads

You can obtain clean kills on cougar without using extremely powerful cartridges. Shooting is quite close, and there is usually no excuse for anything other than perfect shot placement. The skins are fragile, however. A cougar is essentially the size of a small deer, and you can take it cleanly with any deer-sized cartridge. In hound hunting a scoped, high-velocity rifle is really not necessary, and the exit wound from such cartridges can be messy.

To this day the favorite among houndsmen remains a good old lever-action carbine in .30-30. The rifles are light and easy to carry, and the relatively low-velocity bullet will dispatch any cat cleanly without doing a great deal of damage. Some prefer much lighter guns. An outfitter I hunted with in southern British Columbia carried an old slide-action Colt Lightning in .25-20, and insisted that his hunters use it to avoid pelt damage. Handguns are also extremely popular and effective. My old buddy Bob Milek took his cougar very efficiently with one bullet from a .22 magnum revolver, but I personally would prefer a .41 or .44 Magnum.

Bullet Performance

The difficult part isn't killing the cat cleanly. The range is close, and when the cat is treed or bayed, there is usually no reason to rush the shot; you simply don't shoot until you are absolutely certain of a perfect shot. The difficulty is to kill the cat cleanly without damaging the pelt, even though most shots are at more or less point-blank range. Caliber isn't terribly important, but avoid extremely frangible bullets, unless the cartridge is so light that complete penetration is unlikely—like the .22 WMR or .25-20. Expect that the bullet will exit, and understand that a large exit wound is not needed. In rifles, use fairly tough bullets that will exit without a great deal of expansion; in handguns, avoid hollowpoints and use hard-cast, flat-point slugs.

Special Circumstances

If you're hunting cougar by any other method except hounds, things change dramatically. There aren't many successful alternatives, but there are possibilities. A chance encounter is extremely unlikely, but a hunter in cougar country, during open season with a tag in his pocket, can always bump into a cat, and a few do each year. It is almost impossible to bait a cougar, but, rarely, a cougar will come to a varmint call. And it is possible, though extremely difficult, to track a cougar without dogs.

Whether you're tracking or calling or you simply run into a cougar while hunting something else, any shot you can get is a great and rare opportunity. Forget the close-range guns you might use for hound hunting, and carry an accurate, flat-shooting, scoped rifle you can handle well and in which you have absolute confidence.

It is easy to aim too high on the goat because the hump gives an impression of a very deep chest. Take care when placing your shot, as a bullet that hits between the lungs and the spine, or just over the spine, will likely lead to a wounded goat and a long follow-up. (Photo courtesy of Len Rue Jr.)

ROCKY MOUNTAIN GOAT
A tough customer in tough country!

Our mountain goat takes a backseat to the four varieties of wild sheep as a desirable game animal, but for the life of me, I have never understood why. Those who have never hunted goat do not understand the most significant thing about goat hunting, which is that goat country starts where sheep fear to tread. Wild goat tend to inhabit country that is steeper, rougher, and less hospitable than that of wild sheep, and this is generally true of the many types of wild goat the world over.

For hunters there is only one goat, the American mountain goat. Its primary range follows the coastal mountains from Alaska's Kenai Peninsula south to Washington State, and along the spine of the Rockies from British Columbia to Utah. To the north its range thins out quickly, but it is found in diminished density across southern Yukon into the Mackenzies. Introduced herds have also done well in suitable habitat throughout the West, including Colorado, South Dakota's Black Hills, and Alaska's Kodiak Island.

Both males and females grow horns. The nannies often have slightly longer horns, but the billies' horns are much thicker and far more impressive. Males are usually up to 30 percent larger than females, with big billies weighing up to 300 pounds, maybe a bit more. This isn't particularly helpful to know; a nanny with kids is obvious, but it is extremely difficult to judge the size and sex of a lone goat, and mature goats are often loners. Typically, the billies

Goats have a reputation of being both phlegmatic and tough. Mature billies tend to have a large hump, so it is important to place the shot not too high in the chest. With a well-placed bullet, Rocky Mountain goats are not hard to kill. (Photo courtesy of Len Rue Jr.)

have a slightly yellowish cast to their coats; nannies tend to be whiter. This is not definitive, however, especially if there is no snow and the coats are generally dirty. With good optics it is not difficult to see the heavier bases of a really good male, but extremely large nannies and midsize billies can still fool you. The only absolutely foolproof way to tell a male mountain goat from a female is to look at the base of the horns with good optics. This takes patience. Male goats have a black, padlike gland at the rear of the horn bases; females do not.

Hunting season usually opens in late summer in much of goat country. This is a beautiful time to be in the high country, but it's generally a poor time to hunt goat. The animals tend to be in very high, rough country, so you have to climb a lot more to get to them. The real problem, however, is that the mountain goat's summer coat is thin and patchy and makes a poor mount. Later on, when snows come to the high country, the goat will move down—at least a little way. This doesn't necessarily make the hunting easier; you may not have to climb as high, but you'll have to deal with snowy, icy, treacherous slopes. Hunting goat as late as is safely practical is by far the best because by late fall the winter coats are in their full glory—long and soft and luxurious.

Shots at Goat

Wild goat rely heavily on their ability to negotiate the crags. They see well, and there's nothing wrong with their senses of smell and hearing—but up in the rocks they are supremely confident that they can go where no predator can follow. For this reason they are generally not particularly wary or difficult to stalk. Mind you, it is extremely difficult to stalk them from below because their instincts tell them danger is most likely to lie there. If you can get above them and keep the wind in your favor, you are likely to get close enough for a good shot.

It is often purely a problem of terrain. You will see many goat in such rough, horrible stuff that it is either impossible or too doggoned dangerous to get close enough for a shot. You will also see goat that you can easily shoot but that you could not recover without great risk, without technical climbing gear, or both. So if you do enough goat hunting, you will find goat that you simply must walk away from. Unless badly spooked, they are quite habitual, so if you find a good billy in a bad place you can usually find it again, and it might be in a better spot. The bad news is that, if there's enough grass and a bit of water, a goat may stay on the same unreachable ledge for days on end!

Glassing and stalking is the only way to hunt goat. Like all white animals, they can be spotted at tremendous distances before the snow flies. In snow it's a bit more difficult, but their yellowish cast shows up against snow far better than, say, the pure white of a Dall sheep. Once you spot a goat, the secret is to find a safe, sane, and hidden approach that will bring you within range.

Goat are thought of as long-range game, but I have never personally found this to be the case. They live in big, rugged country, so a long shot is always possible, but in my experience the jagged, broken country that goat love usually allows for a fairly close approach. I have hunted numerous varieties of wild goat on four continents. I don't recall ever taking a shot at more than 250 yards, and that just once. I have taken most of my goat within one hundred yards, and on many occasions I have been within twenty-five yards of mountain goat and other varieties of wild goat.

Taking the Shot

Some years ago I hunted goat in the Kootenays of southeastern British Columbia in November, a perfect time to find a great goat. The valleys were still fairly clear, but the slopes were covered with snow, and it was a tough hunt. It got tougher when I just plain missed a perfectly acceptable shot at a great goat. I don't like to miss, so I don't know if it was pure nerves or if I ate something I shouldn't have, but I was extremely sick all that night.

The next morning, shaky and queasy, I forced myself to the top of the mountains. It was windy and extremely cold, but we got the drop on a goat bedded on a little bench about a hundred yards directly below us. It looked to be a good billy, but it was alone, so we couldn't be certain. We held the spotting scope tripod down against the wind and finally resolved the black scent pads behind the black horns. It was a billy, and a long-horned one as well.

I don't like to shoot bedded animals, and on this goat the angle was bad. We elected to wait it out, so I shook and shivered on the top of that windswept ridge for an hour. Finally the goat stood, and I shot it on the shoulder with my David Miller 7mm Remington Magnum, not the most accurate rifle I own but one of the most consistent. Absolutely nothing happened. So I shot it again with the same hold. Still nothing, and then it took a few steps, coming perilously close to a steep chute that would take it to God knows where. I shot again with the same hold, and my goat took a couple more steps and vanished into that chute.

We found it a hundred yards down, stone dead, with a group on its shoulder and on into the heart, measuring little more than an inch. Pound for pound, I have never encountered any animal in the world that is tougher than the mountain goat. It seems exceptionally resistant to bullet shock, with an uncanny ability to simply walk away from a hit that would flatten most animals of similar size right in their tracks.

Mind you, a short run after a fatal shot isn't unusual and should be expected. But with goat this is a problem because of the incredibly rugged terrain they inhabit. Upon sensing danger—danger perhaps meaning the sting of a bullet—a goat will instinctively head for the steepest, nastiest incline it can get to. It might be dead on its feet, but it doesn't know that, and the goat will tumble over a cliff or down a shale slide—perhaps ruining the hide and breaking the horns—and quite possibly will wind up in a spot from which you cannot recover it. So the idea with goat is to stop them and drop them.

I must tell you that I don't know exactly how to do this. Even if you're close enough and the conditions are right for a head or neck shot, you shouldn't try either because, especially with the white cape, you might destroy the trophy. A spine shot is possible, but oh so tricky. A standard lung shot is extremely unlikely to stop a goat before it launches itself over a precipice. The very best option is clearly the shoulder/heart shot. Its placement is the same as with any other animal: Simply follow the centerline of the foreleg into the bottom third of the body. On a broadside presentation this shot will break the on-shoulder, penetrate the heart, and, if everything is perfect, break the off-shoulder as well.

If you take out both shoulders, you have a good chance to drop the animal in its tracks, which is where you want it. But I want to recommend something on goat that I would not recommend on any other animal. Goat are almost always taken within a few yards of a steep incline. With the last breath in its body and that final burst of adrenaline, a goat will make for the vertical slopes that are its natural sanctuary. To get there it will drive with its back legs if it is able, even if both front shoulders are broken. Place your first shot perfectly, and if your goat goes down, fine. If it's making a last run and isn't anywhere close to a cliff or chute, equally fine. But if it's still moving and likely to get into some bad stuff, shoot it high through the hips. This is definitely not a "perfect shot," nor a first shot—but it is the best way to immobilize a goat that has already taken a fatal bullet.

The Right Goat

Under most circumstances both nannies and billies are legal game, for two reasons. It is so difficult to determine the sex of a goat that it would be foolish to regulate otherwise, and goat are so prolific that taking a nanny without kids does little biological harm. The goat with the longest horns are usually nannies, so an exceptionally long-horned nanny can be a very fine trophy. To most hunters, however, the more massive bodies and thick horns of a billy are the superior trophy.

Any billy with horns over nine inches is an acceptable trophy, and any billy with horns over ten inches is outstanding. Depending on mass, a billy with ten-inch horns could make the rigid standards for the Boone and Crockett record book. A billy with eleven-inch horns, which is rare, should easily make it, and the world record is just twelve inches. No one, even with the best optics, can accurately judge mass at the second and third quarters, so there isn't much separating good from great. Ear length of around six inches is a reasonable guide for length, but pay attention to the curve of the horn. The extremely straight horns of most billies probably aren't as long as you think they are, and you will generally get a bit more length than is apparent from a well-curved horn. Unless you're obsessed with having your name in the record book, the best course is to try hard to find a billy goat with horns that are apparently thick and seem to be more than 1½ times longer than the ears. Match this with a thick, luxurious coat, and you will have a great trophy.

Guns and Loads

Any flat-shooting, accurate, and well-scoped rifle from .270 Winchester through the magnum .30s is a fine rifle for goat. In other words, any good sheep rifle is also a great rifle for goat. The country will almost certainly be extremely steep, so gun weight is definitely a factor. Heavy rifles are difficult enough in sheep country, and they have no place on goat mountains.

Bullet Performance

Although goat are extremely tough, I am not convinced that larger calibers are the answer. Goat are slab-sided animals, and, as physically tough as they are, they don't offer a great deal of resistance to a bullet. On goat you want a bullet that will open up quickly and do serious damage to the vital organs. Provided you're shooting an adequate caliber with a bullet that is reasonably heavy-for-caliber, goat aren't so big or heavily boned that you need to worry about failure to penetrate the shoulder. A good old .270 with fast-opening, 130-grain bullets will not only work fine on any goat but will almost certainly work better than a .375 that fires bullets designed for much heavier game. On goat you really don't want tough, penetrating bullets. Think instead about good old conventional softpoints like Sierra, Hornady, Speer, Winchester Power Points, Federal Hi-Shok, and Remington Core-Lokt, or newer polymer-tipped bullets like Nosler Ballistic Tip, Hornady A-Max, Swift Scirocco, and Winchester Ballistic Silvertip. Bullets like these, when mated with a perfect shot, are far more likely to get into the vitals and do the damage necessary to stop a goat before it pitches off into vertical country.

There is a formidable gristle plate on a mature feral hog. A heart or shoulder shot will require the hunter to penetrate that gristle for a humane kill. Unless the situation is dire, a brain shot is not recommended because the target is so small.
(Photo courtesy of Gary Kramer)

Feral Hog

FERAL HOG

Not native, but an all-American game animal just the same!

Years ago, when I was working in Los Angeles, one of the closest, easiest, and least expensive hunting getaways available was to dash up to the Central Coast region and hunt wild hog. Public land is scarce in that region, and public lands that hold wild hog populations are scarcer yet because pigs are naturally drawn to private land where there's agriculture and permanent water. An extended drought in the early 1980s changed things, but in the 1970s there were tons of wild hog in the coastal mountains, and we did pretty well. We would gather around midnight at my house in a northern suburb of Los Angeles, drive north through the wee hours, and hunt our tails off all day—often making the four-hour return trip that night. I figure we averaged about 50 percent success on those grueling "search-and-destroy missions"—not bad for one-day hunts on public land!

In California the wild hog is a full-fledged big-game animal, requiring not only a license but also tags. This is somewhat of a joke because our season is year-round, and there is no bag limit, although residents and nonresidents must purchase tags for each pig. But they are legally a big-game animal in the Golden State and for many years now been more important than deer in terms of both hunter participation and numbers harvested. Elsewhere this full-fledged status is rare, but there are free-ranging populations of wild pig in many parts of the country. They extend from California up into Oregon, and certain river systems

Hunters often underestimate feral hogs. They have tough bones and a super-hard shoulder plate made of gristle. The best, well-constructed bullets should be used, and most guides prefer a caliber of .30-06 or larger. (Photo courtesy of Gary Kramer)

Feral Hog

in Colorado and New Mexico have them. Wild hog are extremely well distributed in Texas, with some now spilling up into Oklahoma. The razorbacks of Arkansas are legendary, and from there wild hog extend southeast—not quite continuously, but close—all the way to Florida. Most of the Hawaiian Islands also have wild hog.

In addition to genuinely wild hog there are "hunting preserves" all over the country that offer hog hunting as a staple. Some of them have breeding populations, offering a hunting experience that differs little from hunting free-range populations. Others, regrettably, are "put and take" situations, offering hunting that is a poor substitute for the great hog hunting thousands of American hunters enjoy.

Our wild hog is often called wild boar, European wild boar, Russian boar, razorback, and even more exotic titles. The Eurasian wild boar—and the good old barnyard domestic pig are actually one and the same species: *Sus scrofa*. The Eurasian wild boar is a massive animal. It is all shoulders and head, with a grizzled grayish-brown coat, long snout, ears that are short and straight, and a straight tail. The young are reddish with white stripes at birth, a telltale sign of pure wild stock in the bloodline. Domestic swine, although conspecific with their wild ancestors, have been bred into a wild array of colors. When the primary bloodlines are from domestic swine, you will see hog that are white, black, gray, brown, red, spotted, belted, and you name it.

In terms of trophy quality, most of us who hunt pig feel that the fairly common black boar and the grizzled Eurasian-type hog make the best-looking head mounts, but there

Feral Hog

isn't really much difference between these "good-looking" pigs and the odd-colored animals you often see. Left to forage for themselves for just a couple of generations, the domestic swine regresses quickly. The shoulders become more powerful and the fat hams streamline. They become hairier, the ears become straight instead of floppy, and the tail unkinks. All boar, domestic and feral, are capable of growing the same wicked tusks, and the boar grow a thick cartilage shield over neck and shoulders, probably protection against other boar during their vicious mating battles.

Size varies tremendously, depending largely on available food. I occasionally hear about "wild hog" that weigh in excess of six hundred pounds. This is certainly possible in the barnyard, so it is theoretically possible in the wild if food conditions are ideal. But not in my country! Our wild hog deal with long dry seasons and periodic food shortages. A nice-size mature boar in our country starts at about 180 pounds, and a genuine 250-pound boar on good scales is big. We do get larger boar; on rare occasions boar will weigh over 300 pounds, and weights up to 350 pounds aren't unheard of.

A mature boar, whether it weighs two hundred pounds or twice that much, is a most formidable creature. The armor plate on its shoulders may be more than an inch thick. It might have as much as four inches of razor-sharp tusk showing above the gum line—and it has no enemies save man and other boar of like size. Mountain lion and coyote take a toll on young pig, which is probably a good thing, because *Sus scrofa* is an extremely prolific breeder. Sows are also somewhat vulnerable, especially just before and after giving birth. A healthy, mature boar, however, is beyond the capability of any North American predator. Although its eyesight is poor, that wide snout is incredibly sensitive, and its ears are almost equally keen. It learns early that humans are dangerous, and its normal reaction on scenting man or hearing a strange noise will be flight. But if it's hurt or cornered, it just might fight.

Shots at Wild Boar

Techniques for hunting pig vary with the area. Hunting wild hog with dogs is probably the most common technique in the southeast, and there are hound hunters in Texas and California. This means extremely close shooting, and it can be fast and quite dangerous. In areas with heavy cover, a lot of hog are taken from stands, not only incidental to deer hunting but also on purpose. In my country we have rolling coastal hills. Some hills and valleys are choked with poison oak, manzanita, and chaparral—ideal bedding cover. Other hillsides are relatively open and studded with acorn-bearing oaks. We call this "oak grassland" country, and it's ideal country to glass and stalk pig, which is my favorite hunting technique.

When stalking pig you can usually get fairly close, but the shooting isn't the point-blank range common with hound hunting. Shots much beyond a hundred yards are uncommon, because you can usually get at least that close. But anytime you're stalking there may be obstacles—brush, shifting wind, moving game—that prevent you from getting as close as you would like. I usually tell hunters to be prepared for shooting up to two hundred yards, and that covers almost all sensible shooting situations.

Feral Hog

The Perfect Shot: Mini Edition for North America II

Typically hog start moving and feeding in the late afternoon, feeding and resting through the night, and then returning to bedding grounds in thick cover in the early morning. Pig tend to move along well-established trails, so in the morning we try to catch them moving from known feeding areas to bedding cover. In the afternoon we often set up closer to bedding cover, hoping the pig will start to move just before dark. On particularly good days I've seen literally hundreds of pig moving, and it isn't unusual to see several groups totaling forty or fifty in a morning or afternoon hunt. Sometimes, of course, the pig just vanish, and sometimes you only see a couple.

Taking the Shot

Wild hog are extremely tough. They are often taken very close to heavy cover, and because of their thick hide and layer of fat, they don't bleed very much. Wounded pig are very difficult to recover, so it's essential to hit them hard. Head and neck shots are certainly good options, but the long shape of a pig's skull makes the placement very tricky for a brain shot. I tend to stay away from it, but if you can hit just in front of and slightly below the ear on a broadside presentation, you will get your pig. The best neck shot is just behind and slightly below the ear, in the center of the first third of the neck. This is also tricky, but it certainly will work.

The standard lung shot is also a bit tricky on pig because a pig's heart and lungs lie a bit farther forward than they do in the deer family, so a very standard behind-the-shoulder lung shot that would be almost immediately fatal on a deer can easily be a bit too far back

Feral Hog

on a pig. The placement is the same. Mentally divide the body into horizontal thirds. On a broadside presentation, come up the back line of the foreleg into the bottom of the middle third. This will be a good lung shot, but the difference is that you have very little margin for error to the rear. Still, this is one of the better shots on a wild hog—especially if it's a big pig and you're shooting a fairly light cartridge.

If you have plenty of gun and plenty of bullets, then a shoulder/heart shot is probably better and certainly safer. Just come up the centerline of the foreleg into the middle of the bottom third of the body. This will probably take out the major arteries at the top of the heart rather than the heart itself, but such a shot will be quickly fatal and offers the greatest margin for error.

The Right Hog

There are two ways to hunt pigs. You can shoot for meat, or you can shoot for a trophy. They aren't mutually exclusive, but a young boar or, even better, a fat sow, offers much better pork than a rank old boar. In my little town we have at least a half-dozen outfitters who make much of their families' income hunting wild hog. They tend to call a big, old boar a "sausage pig," meaning that's all the meat is fit for, while the preferred meat comes from animals weighing about 100 to 125 pounds. I don't necessarily agree. The chops and hams from a boar can be very good, but they need to be smoked. The meat from a smaller pig is very good fresh. Actually, I think our wild hog have better, more flavorful pork than domestic pig, so most of my pig hunting these days is for "meat hogs."

Feral Hog

Now, if you want a trophy, you have three considerations: size, tusks, and color. This is a tall order. It is very difficult to see the tusks on a live pig. Sometimes you'll catch a flash, but often dirt and brush prevent a really close look. Smaller boar can have teeth that are just as good as those of very large boar—and tusks are often broken off short. Body size is much easier to see, and, provided you get a good look in a clear spot, it usually isn't all that difficult to tell a boar from a sow. But color complicates things terribly. To me it isn't that important, but many hunters want only a dark-colored boar for mounting. This may not be the wisest course because really good boar with thick tusks showing 2½ inches or more above the gum line are fairly uncommon. If you see a really big boar, consider it a trophy regardless of color—and if both tusks are long and unbroken, you just got a great bonus!

Guns and Loads

There's a big difference between a hundred-pound meat pig and a really big boar. A .243 is just fine for the former but isn't enough gun for the latter. This doesn't mean you need a cannon. My old buddy Mike Ballew guided hunters to literally thousands of pig during his Dye Creek days. Mike hates big guns and usually carries a .243 or .257 Roberts for all his deer hunting. For backup on pigs he always took out a "big gun," which to him meant a 7x57mm or .270! My local pig-guiding buddies don't all agree. Roger Miller uses his .270 Weatherby Magnum loaded with Barnes X-Bullets. Kyler Hamman usually carries a .375 H&H. August Harden usually carries his 8mm

Remington Magnum. Alfred Luis is another .270 fan, but he recently acquired a .338 Ackley Improved for his pig hunting.

Anything from about .270 on up will work just fine on even the largest pig, but I think something on the order of a .30-06 is probably the best all-round choice. For close-in hunting the good old brush cartridges, like the .35 Remington, .375 Winchester, .444 Marlin, and .45-70, are just wonderful. I like the .35s, and I do most of my hog hunting with the .348 Winchester, .358 Winchester, and .35 Whelen. My most recent "pig gun" is a light .350 Remington Magnum, also a wonderful choice. All of these cartridges will reach out to two hundred yards, but they will also absolutely flatten a pig, whether up close or out there. Handguns are also great for close-range use, especially when hunting with dogs, but you should consider no less a pistol cartridge than the .44 Magnum.

Bullet Performance

Again, there's a big difference between a small meat hog and a big boar. You never know when a huge boar with gleaming tusks might appear, so you need a bullet that will absolutely penetrate, no matter what size pig appears. I believe strongly in bullets designed to penetrate, especially if you're using fairly light cartridges (like typical deer rifles). Good bullets include the Nosler Partition, Barnes X-Bullet, Swift A-Frame, Trophy Bonded Bear Claw, and Winchester Fail Safe. No bullet is forgiving of shot placement, but all of these bullets will get into the vitals where it counts.

The javelina is small with a light bone structure. Any deer caliber will result in a quick, humane kill. (Photo courtesy of Len Rue Jr.)

JAVELINA
Our smallest big game . . .

The javelina is a fearsome-looking creature, all head and teeth, and when threatened it pops its teeth together and makes a truly frightening noise. Normally, it is found in small herds of a half-dozen to fifteen or so, but once in a while you run into much larger groups. Javelina have a fierce reputation, and there are stories of humans being "treed" for hours by large groups of these ferocious creatures. Despite its intimidating appearance and the sound effects of its teeth clashing together, the javelina is really a very small creature. Normal weight for mature javelina is no more than forty pounds. Males and females are about the same size, and the occasional outsized specimen will top fifty pounds.

Because of its flat snout and piglike shape, we tend to refer to the javelina as a "pig," but it really isn't. Its proper name is collared peccary. The Brazilian Indians gave it the name peccary, which means "an animal that makes many paths through the woods." Collared refers to the light-colored stripe running diagonally from shoulder to throat, generally distinct against the grizzled gray coat. Its Latin name has bounced back and forth, but today it is generally agreed to be *Tayassu tajacu*, *tayassu* meaning "gnawer of roots" in an Indian tongue and *tajacu* taken from a native Brazilian word for this animal.

There are two species of javelina: the collared peccary and the white-lipped peccary. The collared peccary is hunted in Texas, New Mexico, and Arizona. The white-lipped peccary

Javelina

Unlike its distant cousin the wild boar, the javelina is a light-boned and easily killed quarry. Any caliber from .223 on up, with sensible bullet construction, will do. (Photo courtesy of Len Rue Jr.)

Javelina

ranges from the jungles of southern Mexico down through Central America. It is more uniformly dark in color with a pale lower jaw (for which it is named), and it is considerably larger, weighing as much as eighty-five pounds. The giant of the breed is the Chaco peccary, which is similar in color to the collared peccary but with longer, paler hair on the ears and legs. This giant is considered a different species (*Catagonus wagneri*).

Despite similarities in appearance, the peccaries are considerably different from true pigs. The feet are different, the stomach is different, there is no gall bladder, and the teeth are considerably different. The tusks of a peccary are elongated canines that grow more or less straight; a pig's tusks grow up and out. Javelina also have a prominent scent gland about six inches up from the stubby tail, giving the animals a strong odor that, in heavy cover, acts as a sure giveaway of their presence.

In good country javelina can be extremely plentiful, which is misleading. They are not nearly as prolific as pigs; the females usually bear no more than two young. Although they do well in arid country, they do need water, so their populations suffer during drought years. These factors have led to more restrictive hunting of collared peccary in the United States.

Shots at Javelina

Hunting techniques vary considerably, depending on where you are. In game-rich Texas the javelina receives little respect as a game animal and tends to be hunted coincidentally to deer hunting, or simply ignored. Javelina are extremely

Javelina

79

common in the brush country of south Texas, but it is very difficult to hunt them on purpose there. They are occasionally hunted with dogs, and they will respond to a varmint call. More often, however, they are taken when they wander by a deer stand. (This "wandering by" is considerably aided by the fact that baiting for deer is legal in Texas.) Shots will be close and fast when calling or hunting with dogs. In contrast, a shot from a deer stand is defined as any shot the hunter believes he or she can make!

Once you get out of the thick brush and the country starts to open up, the situation changes. Along the oak mottes of the coastal plains, the oak-studded ridges of the Edwards Plateau, and anywhere you can find prickly pear flats, you have an opportunity to glass and stalk javelina. Farther west, in New Mexico and Arizona and down through Sonora, you tend to find javelina up in hilly country where glassing and stalking are the primary hunting techniques.

In Arizona most javelina seasons occur in the spring, and the spring "pig" season is a major event. Part of the reason is that wildlife resources are fragile in Arizona's arid country, so virtually all big-game tags are by drawing, and many hopeful residents do not draw deer tags. Part of the reason is that the season is in the early spring when not much else is going on in the hunter's world—and this is a glorious time to be in the southwestern mountains.

I have not hunted javelina in New Mexico, but I have hunted them in Texas, Arizona, and Sonora, and I have enjoyed every minute of it. The primary challenge is to find them, and although they are generally not scarce, they are small animals that live in very big country. When glassing, you look for small black peppercorns on a distant hillside. It doesn't take much brush to hide them, but when they step into the open they appear shiny and black and are quite easy to see.

Sometimes you hunt them by sound. Although their family groups tend to be quite social, they seem to have a lot of extremely vocal arguments, so it's easy to hear them. Javelina also have extremely keen noses, and their hearing is just fine, but they can't see worth beans. This means that, provided you watch the wind, it usually isn't too difficult to close in for a shot once you locate the game. This makes them excellent game for bow hunters, and I've long enjoyed hunting them with a pistol. Depending on the country, you can also snipe at them at long range, but I've always enjoyed closer encounters—and just because you are close doesn't necessarily mean the shots will be easy.

Taking the Shot

Although small, javelina are fairly tough. If the shot is placed poorly, they can take the impact of surprisingly powerful cartridges and escape into the brush. Record-book entries are based on skull measurements, and the bleached skull of a javelina makes a really neat secondary trophy, so avoid head shots. The neck shot is OK; just shoot right into the center of the neck—but it is a very small target. The lung shot and the shoulder/heart shot are by far the best. The animal is small enough that there isn't much margin for error no matter what you do, so I recommend coming up the centerline of the leg almost halfway into the body.

The Perfect Shot: Mini Edition for North America II

The Right Javelina

Boone and Crockett does not have a category for collared peccary, but Safari Club International does. Trophies are accepted into the record book based on skull measurement, but this is impossible to judge on a live animal. To me, one javelina looks much the same as another. Brush usually prevents me from getting a glimpse of the sex organs, and without that I've never been able to tell the males from the females reliably. Fortunately, no open javelina season requires that you shoot only boars, so most of the time the goal is to find the biggest javelina you can. They are herd animals, and this is the good news because the best way to judge size is simply to compare them and shoot the one that looks the biggest.

Actually, unless you want to mount the trophy, a little boar is probably just the right size to shoot. Young javelina aren't great eating, but they're edible. The adults aren't very good at all. This creates quite a dilemma: I like hunting javelina, but I don't like to eat them, and I don't want to mount another one—so it has actually been some years since I've shot one.

Guns and Loads

I have taken a lot of javelina with rifles, but I have taken more with handguns. Javelina are actually quite easy to hunt, and there isn't much challenge involved in killing one with a scoped centerfire rifle. Of course, you don't really know that until you've taken a couple. I'm certainly not knocking hunting them with rifles, but alternative means—whether handgun, bow, or muzzleloader—offer a more satisfying experience.

Javelina

Javelina

Whether you prefer a rifle or a handgun, it's ridiculous to talk about "adequate cartridges" on an animal weighing no more than fifty pounds. Any centerfire rifle is clearly "adequate," but if I were choosing a rifle for javelina, I would use the milder .22 centerfires, from .22 Hornet up through .223 Remington. In handguns any cartridge from the .357 magnum upward will do just fine. I have shot more javelina with a .44 Magnum revolver than with anything else, but that's because I like the .44 and that's what I usually carry, not because that level of power is essential. The scope-sighted "specialty pistols" chambered to rifle cartridges are also lots of fun. I have used the 6mm Benchrest Remington in an XP-100 to take a number of javelina during Arizona's HAM (Handgun, Archery, Muzzleloader) seasons, and it works just fine—but a single-shot pistol in .223 Remington would work just as well.

Bullet Performance

A fast-opening bullet from a powerful cartridge, whether fired from a rifle or pistol, can really make a mess of a javelina. Since adequate power isn't really an issue, I recommend using fairly tough bullets that will simply zip on through without doing a lot of unnecessary damage. In revolvers, hard-cast, flat-point bullets are probably a better choice than destructive hollowpoints; in rifles, think about controlled-expansion designs instead of frangible bullets that will blow up. I mentioned that I like the .22 centerfires for javelina, but you will get better results and less trophy damage if you use them with heavy-for-caliber bullets intended for deer-size game instead of the more common and more destructive varmint bullets.

With lots of hair just about everywhere, it is not easy to see where to aim on a muskox. If possible, follow the animal's front leg straight up to find the heart/lung area. (Photo courtesy of Leonard Lee Rue III)

MUSKOX
Beware of the hair!

The recovery of the muskox in the far northern regions during the latter half of the past century is a great conservation success story. Arctic explorers found plenty of the shaggy beasts, but as the Arctic was opened up, hunters, trappers, and Inuit hunted them for meat, hides, and the soft layer of underwool called *qiviut*. Its numbers declined dramatically during the latter half of the nineteenth and the first couple of decades of the twentieth century. With protection, however, its numbers have increased dramatically. Today Northwest Territories may have as many as fifty thousand muskox. The animals also remain plentiful in eastern Greenland, and transplanted populations have been established in Alaska, Norway, Siberia, and northern Quebec.

Although fairly large on the scale of North American big game, the muskox is a relatively small wild ox, with bulls normally weighing around seven hundred pounds. Their appearance is deceiving; they look much larger than they are because of the incredibly long hair that enables them to survive Arctic winters. Both males and females have horns that grow close to the head, turn out, and then curve upward in sharp hooks. At first it seems difficult to tell the sexes apart, but only the bulls have horns with heavy bosses, and the two horns are almost joined together at the top of the skull. Coloration is generally dark brown, with a lighter saddle patch on the flanks and pale legs.

There is a lot of hump and loose, curtainlike, guard hair on a muskox. This gives the animal's body an appearance of being much larger than it actually is. (Photo courtesy of Leonard Lee Rue III)

Although not all authorities agree, they generally recognize that there are two subspecies: *Ovibos moschatus moschatus*, the barren ground muskox of mainland Canada, and *Ovibos moschatus wardi*, the Greenland muskox. The barren ground muskox is definitely larger in the body, and record-book listings suggest that it grows somewhat larger horns. Greenland muskox are found not only in Greenland but also on Canada's offshore islands; the transplanted herd on Nunivak Island is Greenland muskox. Boone and Crockett currently lumps the two subspecies together; Safari Club's record book separates them into different categories.

Shots at Muskox

Along Canada's northern shores you can find muskox in open tundra rich with lichen and fingers of scrub willow. The muskox are better fed, and they grow larger. Mainland bulls are said to run up to 750 pounds, but friends who have hunted them there maintain that really big bulls are considerably heavier. The Arctic Islands are much more barren and are also fairly arid, with limited snowfall and sparse grass that seems insufficient to support such a large animal. Here body weights for mature bulls are unlikely to exceed 650 pounds. Wherever it lives, the muskox inhabits big, open country.

Most muskox hunting takes place in late fall and early spring when the landscape is white and its dark, bulky form can be seen at vast distances. A hunter will often encounter a solitary bull, but muskox are gregarious creatures and usually occur in small herds of ten to twenty.

The Perfect Shot: Mini Edition for North America II

They have a tough time making a living, so they're usually active during the day. You will often find them out on windswept flats, digging through the snow to graze.

Weather is the primary enemy. My first muskox hunt was in November when the days were extremely short and the cold was incredible. It started to gray up around ten o'clock in the morning, and around midday the sun came over the horizon in a short arc. It was pitch-dark again and very cold by three in the afternoon. We came upon a fair-size herd late in the afternoon of our first hunting day. I figured I would pass the shot because it was too early in the hunt. When my guides realized this, they became concerned, telling me they didn't know what the weather might do and maybe this was our best chance. I shot the largest bull in the herd, and it turned out to be huge. The next day bad weather set in, and visibility went to zero! The message is, on this hunt, you must make hay while the sun shines!

Historically, the shaggy beast's only enemy was wolves, and the muskox would form a circle, horns outboard, in defense. When modern muskox hunting first opened, this was also their defense against humans, so it wasn't much of a hunt. The animals would make a circle, and all you needed to do was walk around the herd, locate the bulls, and take your shot as soon as the chosen bull was clear. These days you will occasionally see this, but muskox have now been hunted enough that they know the difference between men and wolves. They are much more likely to run than to stand, so today you need to glass them from farther away and make a covered approach within shooting range. Either way, muskox hunting is not difficult, nor are the shots likely to be difficult. The primary problem is the cold.

You should, however, not underrate the potential danger of hunting muskox. Muskox have the equipment, the power, and occasionally the disposition to turn the tables. Their defensive circle once formed allows individual animals to charge outward from the circle toward the perceived danger, then retreat into the press. Bow hunters especially can make the mistake of getting too close. A few years ago Otis Chandler, an extremely experienced hunter, got well and truly hammered by a muskox bull that refused to leave its buddy after Chandler shot it. He survived despite numerous broken bones—but I can imagine few things less pleasant than being badly hurt in that cold.

Taking the Shot

You will travel mostly on snow machines or on sleds behind the machines. This allows you to cover quite a lot of ground, and if the weather is perfect, you may be able to look at a lot of muskox. Because the country is so open, there is certainly the opportunity for a long shot, but muskox are rarely so spooky that it's necessary. Most of the time it isn't difficult to close within a hundred yards, so there is no excuse for less than a perfect shot.

The heaviest layer of hair is underneath the body, and that makes it almost impossible to see where the hair stops and the muskox starts. It's extremely easy to shoot too low, and I did exactly that with my first muskox. On an animal as big as a muskox, the shoulder/heart shot is definitely the best approach. On most animals you simply come up the centerline of the foreleg to the bottom third of the body, but on muskox there's a good chance you'll hit only hair, or at best the foreleg itself. Instead, come up the centerline of the foreleg fully halfway between what appears to be the belly line and the back line. Chances are this placement will actually be low in the chest where you want it, but it will not be too high.

The Right Bull

Muskox are quite difficult to judge, and because the weather is so uncertain you may not get many chances. Boone and Crockett measures the length of each horn, the width of each boss, width at the first quarter, and circumferences at the second and third quarters. SCI uses total length of horns, from tip to tip across the bosses, and width of the bosses. By either measurement a big muskox is a big muskox—but neither measurement is particularly easy to judge. Look for horns that go down below the jaw before turning up, with hooks that come up as far as possible. The bosses are extremely important by either system, so look for a huge, bronze skullcap. If the boss appears to be partly covered by hair, it probably isn't very big.

In spite of today's increased standards, the muskox remains one of the easiest animals to get into the hallowed B&C record book. Not all will make it, but if the weather gives you a chance to look around, your odds are better with muskox than with any other animal. Record-book score, however, shouldn't be the most important thing. The high Arctic is so different that it might as well be a different planet. It's beautiful, especially on a clear day, and the night skies are spectacular, especially if you catch the Northern Lights. The trophy is spectacular, too, and the fabulously long hair is every bit as impressive as the horns.

Guns and Loads

The muskox is a big, blocky animal, but not so big as to require extremely powerful rifles. I used an 8mm Remington Magnum on my first muskox, and it worked just fine. I used a .375 Weatherby Magnum for my second, and it was spectacular. But, in truth, any versatile cartridge from .30-06 on up to the .33s will work well. The rifle should be scoped, but it should also wear auxiliary iron sights because rifles take an incredible pounding on the sleds and snow machines.

The most important consideration is to weatherproof the rifle completely. Liquid lubricants absolutely will freeze, so I strongly recommend a bolt-action rifle. It is the easiest action to degrease, and it will operate very smoothly with just a bit of dry graphite lubricant. Take the bolt completely apart and degrease it with alcohol or some other degreasing agent. Failure to do this invites a slow hammer fall, or failure to fire altogether.

Bullet Performance

The muskox require bullets that will absolutely penetrate. Just how tough a bullet you should use depends somewhat on the caliber and bullet weight. If you're using fairly light calibers like the 7mm Remington Magnum or .30-06, you have enough gun, but you should use plenty of bullet—bullets that are heavy-for-caliber and tough, like the Barnes X-Bullet, Winchester Fail Safe, and Swift A-Frame. Larger calibers are much more forgiving of bullet performance, but the muskox is simply too large for light, fast, quick-expanding bullets.

Bighorn sheep are not overly tough; however, it is still necessary to place the bullet properly. The point of aim for the lung shot is indicated. (Photo courtesy of Len Rue Jr.)

BIGHORN SHEEP
There's a lot riding on the shot!

To me the bighorn—a dramatic creature with wondrously thick horns—symbolizes the great mountain ranges of the American West. We call them bighorns not for the length of their horns—those of our thinhorn Dall and Stone sheep are actually longer—but for the tremendous mass of the horns. The base circumference on bighorns averages a couple of inches more than on Dall and Stone sheep. Good mature rams approach sixteen inches in basal circumference and occasionally exceed seventeen inches. This weight carries through the quarters quite well, but length is rarely extreme. The horns of bighorns typically curl tighter to the skull, unlike those of thinhorns, which tend to curl around and out.

As with all true horned animals, the horn continues to grow outward from the base throughout the animal's life. When bighorns approach or reach full curl, the horns start to interfere with the rams' peripheral vision, and they rub or broom them against rocks. Thus, at maturity, most bighorns have tips that are thick and worn, increasing the mass at the last quarter. This is part of the character of a good trophy.

There is just one species of bighorn sheep, *Ovis canadensis*, which has several subspecies. Traditionally, hunters have divided them into two groups: the big-bodied, darker-pelaged Rocky Mountain bighorn and the smaller-bodied, lighter-colored sheep adapted to life in the arid Southwest—the desert bighorns.

Rocky Mountain bighorn tend to be somewhat larger than the sheep farther north. Even so, the bighorn is not a large animal when compared to some of the other North American ungulates. A good quality, nonpremium softpoint bullet will do well on broadside shots like this one. (Photo courtesy of Len Rue Jr.)

Bighorn Sheep

The Rocky Mountain bighorn, *Ovis canadensis canadensis*, originally occurred in huge numbers from northern New Mexico, north along the Front Range all through the Rocky Mountain chain, and west to the Sierra Nevadas. Today there are very few "low-country" bighorns, but aggressive reintroductions have restored bighorn populations to suitable high-country habitat in all the Rocky Mountain states and western South Dakota.

The Rocky Mountain bighorn is a big-bodied sheep, and mature rams often exceed three hundred pounds. Note that some of this weight is tied up in the horns—the fresh skull and horns of a really large bighorn can weigh more than forty pounds! Its pelage ranges from gray-brown to very dark, with a white nose patch, white on the back of the front legs and the inside of the back legs, and a large white rump patch surrounding the short dark tail.

Traditionally, the smaller California bighorn (*Ovis canadensis californiana*) has been lumped with the Rocky Mountain sheep for record-keeping purposes. Typically, the California bighorn is about 20 percent smaller in body. Its horns are shorter and less massive and typically grow with more outward flare, so a mature California bighorn is less likely to have broomed tips. California bighorns are also paler in body. Formerly, they ranged from south-central British Columbia and south along the mountain chains to northern California. In addition to native-range herds in British Columbia, Washington, Oregon, Nevada, and California, California bighorn have been transplanted in southwestern Idaho and western North Dakota. Most of these states and provinces also have herds of either desert sheep or Rocky Mountain bighorn, so there are some areas where the subspecies intergrade.

The Perfect Shot: Mini Edition for North America II

There are actually four subspecies that we call desert sheep, all much smaller and paler than the northern bighorns. Body size on mature desert sheep rams runs much less than two hundred pounds. Skulls, ears, the whole works are scaled down from the Rocky Mountain sheep—except that, on the very best rams, the horns aren't actually that much smaller. The new Boone and Crockett world-record Rocky Mountain bighorn was taken in Alberta, scoring 208 ⅜—a huge ram. Surprisingly, the world-record desert bighorn measures 205⅛—imagine how horns like that would look on such a small sheep!

Nelson's bighorn (*Ovis canadensis nelsoni*) is the most widespread of the desert bighorns. It is found from New Mexico to California, and there is an introduced herd in southwestern Colorado. From southern Arizona to Sonora the subspecies is *Ovis canadensis mexicana*. Mexico's Baja Peninsula has two subspecies, *Ovis canadensis cremnobates* in the north and *Ovis canadensis weemsi* at the southern tip.

You might think that bighorns are harder to spot than northern sheep because their coloration offers much better camouflage. This is true to a degree, but the white rump acts like a signpost. The sheep aren't always facing away, but at some point one will turn its rump to you—and you can glass this white circle at incredible distances.

Shots at Bighorns

As with all sheep hunting, hunting a bighorn is largely a matter of painstaking glassing in the right habitat. The primary difference between hunting bighorns and hunting the northern sheep is that there is much more vegetation in bighorn habitat, so it's more difficult to locate sheep unless they're up and feeding. Today most bighorns are found where there are timbered slopes or pockets of heavy timber. The sheep bed in the timber where it's almost impossible to spot them. Even if you know they're there, it's usually unwise to go in after them because bighorns are herd animals, and usually the ram you want is in a band. If you go into close cover after them, there are so many sets of eyes that the chances of getting a shot at the right ram are slim.

Like all sheep, bighorns tend to be most active in the evening; morning movement is somewhat more limited. You need to find them while they're feeding in the meadows and sagebrush pockets above timberline or on the open fingers between the timbered draws, and then plan an appropriate stalk. They bed in the open as well, especially later in the fall when the weather cools down. In November the bighorns rut, and all bets are off. Like all animals, bighorns lose their caution during this period, and the big rams are much more visible as they wander in search of ewes.

The vegetation is much different for desert bighorns, but the hunting is not. They live in desert mountains—very much a living desert, with tall cacti, scrub oak, and mesquite. All of this can easily hide armies of small-bodied sheep. You need to locate desert sheep while they're moving and feeding, and in their warmer climate this movement is often restricted. The bonus is that, because the vegetation is sparser and more scattered, it is much more likely that you can bed a desert bighorn and move in on it. You may not actually shoot it in its bed, but you can discover exactly where it is and get in position. After that it's only a matter of waiting until it moves.

Bighorns have exceptional eyes. They also have keen noses, and they can hear perfectly well, so you need to keep the wind in your favor and be stealthy in your approach. However, virtually throughout their range, sheep hunting is so limited and tightly controlled that, if anything, most bighorn bands are actually less wary than Dall and Stone sheep. And no wild sheep are naturally as wary as our various deer. The hard part is finding the ram you want, but if you find it, there will usually be enough cover to allow an approach within reasonable rifle range. In other words, though a long shot is always a possibility in any mountain hunting, most shots at bighorns are well within three hundred yards. If you can locate a ram that meets your standards, you should be able to get a shot at it.

Taking the Shot

A Rocky Mountain ram is big enough that you must give some consideration to its body mass when you choose cartridges and bullets. However, wild sheep are not particularly strong or tough. A solid hit into the chest cavity will drop, in short order, any ram that ever lived. The problem is that opportunities to hunt any breed of bighorn sheep are so scarce today and the price so high that hunters experience great pressure with any shot.

On any bighorn, forget the fancy stuff about brain, neck, or spine shots. As in most cases, I prefer the lung shot because it offers by far the largest vital target and the most room for error. On a broadside presentation, divide the body horizontally into thirds. Follow the back line of the foreleg up into the body, and shoot the ram in the bottom half of the middle third. The other option, as always, is the shoulder shot. Follow the centerline of the foreleg upward, and place your shot at the top of the bottom third. True broadside presentations are rare, so you must visualize where the vitals lie in relation to the shot angle you have.

The Right Ram

Horn size varies, and as is always the case with trophy quality, horn size partly depends on genetics, feed, and minerals, but it's also a matter of the way a given herd is managed. Some states are extremely conservative in the number of permits they offer; others are more liberal. Bighorn tags are so hard to come by that, unless your budget is absolutely unlimited, you should plan on filling your tag with a ram representative of the area in which you are hunting. Do your research to learn what that means in the area you will be hunting. It would be a shame to shoot a mediocre ram in an area that produces really great sheep. It would be an equal shame to waste the tag by passing good rams for the while searching for the monster that may not exist where you are hunting.

However, that doesn't mean "any legal bighorn" is a good ram in marginal areas. In most states a legal bighorn is a three-quarter-curl ram. Such a ram may be a ten-year-old monarch with heavy bases and massive, broomed tips, or it may be a 3½-year-old youngster, skinny in the bases and still carrying its sharp lamb tips. The former is a trophy ram anywhere bighorns are hunted—but in some areas you might pass it and do better. The latter, in my view, is not yet a bighorn sheep. A trophy is in the eye of the beholder, but to me a bighorn must have mass and character.

Bighorn Guns and Loads

Sheep aren't hard to put down, so large calibers aren't really necessary. Long shots generally aren't necessary, either, but you need to be prepared for them. Traditional sheep rifles like the .270 Winchester and .280 Remington are ideal: adequate in power, able to handle almost any potential shooting situation, and easily tailored into a light, trim package, which is important in a sheep rifle. However, there's another school of thought.

On my first bighorn hunt I used a .270 Winchester, and it was ideal for the shot I got. Several days earlier I had seen that same ram, and I would have taken it then, but we were pinned down on the far side of a sagebrush flat while the sheep rested quietly about four hundred yards away. I didn't feel comfortable taking that shot with a .270, so we waited, hoping the rams would move. They did, but it was too late, and we lost them in the dark. When I drew my second tag, I carried a .300 Weatherby Magnum, and I felt prepared.

Those tags are so precious that the rifle must be right: It's got to be the most accurate, most dependable, flattest-shooting rig you own that you have confidence in and that is light enough for you to carry all day in the mountains . . . and any sheep rifle needs a good scope. A 3–9X is plenty of power, but there's no harm in more powerful variables like the 4.5–14X.

Bighorn Sheep

Bullet Performance

I like a bullet that expands well so that the vital organs are wrecked and the ram goes down as quickly as possible. With sheep I generally use fairly quick-opening bullets, but I ensure penetration by using relatively heavy-for-caliber slugs. I have taken most of my wild sheep with conventional softpoints from Sierra and Hornady, and with polymer-tipped bullets like the Nosler Ballistic Tip. All of these bullets open relatively fast, which is good on sheep—but I don't use light-for-caliber bullets. In my .270 I shoot 140-grain bullets rather than the traditional 130-grain slugs, in 7mm I usually shoot 160-grain bullets, and in the .30s I use 180-grain bullets. I have taken several rams with strongly angled "raking" shots—including my first bighorn and a larger-bodied Marco Polo argali—and adequate penetration has never been an issue.

Special Circumstances

Almost by definition, all shots at bighorns are "special circumstances." The opportunity to hunt these creatures is precious. I drew for twenty years before receiving my first bighorn tag, and I have now applied for desert sheep for nearly thirty years without drawing one. In all hunting, the goal is to make the "perfect shot." A well-placed shot is a moral responsibility, and it equates to a home run with all bases loaded in the bottom of the ninth inning or a winning touchdown as the final buzzer sounds. With bighorns, making that perfect shot is even more important because the opportunity to attempt that shot may never come again in your life.

*When at a steep angle like this one,
it is easy to shoot too far back. The
point of aim, from top to bottom, on
this Stone sheep is:* lung, shoulder,
heart. (Photo courtesy of Leonard
Lee Rue III)

THIN-HORNED SHEEP
Harder to come by every year!

Widely regarded as two entirely different sheep, the snow-white Dall sheep and salt-and-pepper Stone sheep are actually races, or subspecies, of the same wild sheep, *Ovis dalli*. The white sheep, *Ovis dalli dalli*, inhabit the mountain ranges of Alaska, northern Yukon, and the Mackenzie district of the Northwest Territories, and a band of pure-white sheep dips into extreme northwestern British Columbia. Many of us think the dark Stone sheep are named for the gray rocks they live in. Actually, *Ovis dalli stonei* is named in honor of an early naturalist named Stone.

Stone and Dall sheep interbreed, so there is an overlap of these two races. In northern B.C., Stone sheep tend to be quite dark, and some bands of very dark sheep range up into south-central Yukon. But the intergrade area is quite large, and the two subspecies interbreed freely. Where white sheep and dark sheep meet, individual animals can range from pure white to fairly dark, and everything in-between. A classic hybrid is mostly white with a distinctive dark "saddle patch" on the flanks. This is the Fannin sheep, now recognized as an intergrade.

The horns of the Dall and Stone sheep are similar. They are generally golden, with relatively thin horns (compared to bighorns) that usually make a full curl and then flare outward as the ram matures. On average, Stone sheep are slightly bigger-bodied than Dall sheep, and the biggest Stone rams grow slightly larger horns than the biggest Dall rams—probably because Stone sheep have

*A flat-shooting, medium-light caliber
is adequate for Stone sheep as well as
Rocky Mountain goat, which are often
encountered on the same hunt.* (Photo
courtesy of Leonard Lee Rue III)

better nutrition and milder winters in their more southerly mountains. The record books endeavor to keep things simple: A pure white sheep is a Dall sheep, and a sheep with dark hair is a Stone sheep. We can assume this refers to the intergrade area of the Yukon because well into Alaska it is not unusual to find Dall sheep with some dark hairs here and there!

The hunting of the two varieties is essentially the same. Hunters painstakingly glass until they locate a suitable ram and then plan a stalk that will keep them out of sight until they are within shooting range. Sheep can hear quite well, and there's nothing wrong with their noses. However, they rely mostly on their keen eyesight. Rolling rocks are part of their lives, so absolute silence is not as essential as it is when hunting other species. Human voices and the rattling of equipment are taboo, but if you can keep out of sight and keep the wind more or less favorable, it is usually possible to approach your quarry.

One of the main differences between hunting Dall and Stone sheep is that Dall sheep are much easier to spot. Their northern mountains tend to have sparser vegetation, and nothing shows up as well as a pure white sheep; you can see their brilliant white bodies at incredible distances. The darker Stone sheep are considerably more difficult to spot. After the snow flies, the white sheep are camouflaged while darker sheep stand out.

Sheep hunting involves getting to a high vantage point then letting good optics do the looking, but there are various ways of attaining those vantage points. In most Stone sheep country, horseback hunting is traditional; it is also common in the Yukon, and there are a couple of horse outfitters in Alaska. Most Dall sheep hunting is by backpack hunting on

Dall sheep are identical in body size to Stone sheep, and both animals can be hunted well with cartridges in the .270, 7mm, and .308 class of calibers. (Photo courtesy of Leonard Lee Rue III) foot. Nowhere is it particularly common to simply ride up on a ram, jump off, and shoot. It happens, but most likely you will reach a point where you must tie the horses and climb on foot into the real sheep country. You can cover a lot of country on horseback, and a packhorse can carry more and better supplies and can also pack out the game, but eventually you must go back to the horses. Backpack hunting is a fine way to hunt sheep, but you are limited by your physical condition and the amount of food you can carry.

Shots at Thinhorns

The common belief is that sheep hunting is a game for long-range shooting, but extremely long shooting isn't all that common. The difficult part about sheep hunting is climbing into their country and locating a suitable ram. If you can find a ram, you can probably find a way to shoot it. Sometimes it will be a long poke, but usually the mountains have enough ridges and furrows to allow a reasonably close approach.

In the Northwest Territories we stalked a Dall ram on a series of descending benches, taking it from about sixty yards. This shooting distance is not unusual, but with a centerfire rifle there is no reason to push too close and risk spooking the ram. So, the world over, most of my shots at wild sheep have come between 150 and 300 yards—not really a tall order for a reasonably flat-shooting rifle with a good scope.

Patience is often the key. Sheep move a little bit in the early morning but bed most of the day, with their peak movement usually during the late afternoon and early evening hours. If you can bed a ram in the morning, you have all day to work to it. Depending on the situation, you may also be able to predict with some accuracy where it will move when it starts to feed. In the evening you often have a scramble on your hands as you try to close on a ram before it gets dark. Sometimes you have a choice between a longer shot in failing light or trying again in the morning. Sheep usually don't move a great deal during full darkness, so if you locate a ram in late evening you have a very good chance of relocating it at daylight, when you have plenty of time to make a good approach.

Taking the Shot

Wild sheep are not particularly tough creatures, and there are no special considerations in planning the perfect shot. Because almost all wild sheep are taken as trophies, you should avoid brain or neck shots, not only because of the obvious difficulty but also because you could ruin the valuable and nearly irreplaceable cape. I personally prefer the behind-the-shoulder lung shot because wild sheep offer the very best of all wild meat, and a lung shot causes the least meat damage. It also places the shot far enough back to cause minimal damage to the cape. Wild sheep tend to have an obvious "pocket" just behind the shoulder. Look for it just above the back line of the rear foreleg and place your shot about one-third up the body. No wild sheep will walk away from this shot.

There is an exception. Wild sheep are properly creatures of the high basins and meadows, but they will cross through and often bed in extremely rough, rocky places. If there is any chance that your ram will drop into a crevasse or roll off a cliff, think hard before you shoot. You don't want your ram bouncing down a thousand-foot cliff, ruining the meat, horns, and cape, and possibly lodging in a spot from which you can't recover it without great risk. Shoot it carefully on the center of the shoulder, one-third up the body, so you will break heavy bone as well as wreck the vital organs. Even better, look for a broadside presentation so you can break both shoulders—and by all means shoot again if it isn't down!

One note on shooting any white animal: Blood stains the cape badly. Remove the cape as quickly as possible and use cold water to wash out as much of the blood as possible. There will almost always be clear, cold streams in northern sheep country.

The Right Ram

Historically, the magic number for both Dall and Stone sheep was a ram with horns over 40 inches around the curl. These days Stone rams over 40 inches are rare, even with very limited quotas and frightening prices for outfitted hunts. Hunters are taking big rams, both in the classic country in British Columbia and in the Yukon, where the few outfitters who have dark sheep are trying to meet the greatly increased demand for sheep hunting—but not everybody is going to get one. These days you should consider a mature ram from 34 to 39 inches a very fine Stone ram, unless you're willing to go home empty-handed and try again another year.

The chances of getting a big Dall sheep are somewhat better. Part of the reason is that Dall sheep occupy a much larger range, so there are many more options. Most of the Dall sheep country in the Yukon and in the Mackenzie Mountains of the Northwest Territories is still very lightly hunted. Neither is likely to be a good place to get a ram that is genuinely over the magic 40-inch mark, although such sheep surely exist. On the other hand, both areas are good places to get an old ram with mass, character, and horns in the upper thirties.

Alaska's more accessible ranges are hard hunted today. There are lots of sheep, but most full-curl rams are in the 32- to 35-inch class, and older, bigger rams are fairly scarce. This is not universally true. Sheep in the remote Brooks Range tend to be a bit smaller and thinner-horned due to the extreme climate, but there are many good rams, so good trophies are possible. Perhaps the biggest Dall sheep today are available in the rough, tough ranges of southern Alaska, especially the Chugach. A nice full-curl Dall ram is a beautiful trophy and is not that difficult to come by, but if you want a really big ram today you'll work hard, and probably more than once.

Guns and Loads

Dall and Stone sheep are good-size animals. Fall weights of mature rams run from about 180 pounds to as much as 250 pounds, though the latter is rare. These sheep are not as large as the biggest whitetail or mule deer buck—nor, in my opinion, are they nearly as tough. Though you need to be able to take longer shots if necessary, you don't need a cannon to hunt sheep. From the standpoint of caliber alone, something on the order of a .25-06 would be just fine, and some sheep hunters prefer the fast .25s.

Personally, though, I want a bit more gun. You will work very hard for any shot you get at a wild sheep, and you should be prepared to take any reasonable shot that is within your capabilities. Somewhat larger calibers not only give you more energy and bullet weight but also buck the wind a bit better. The faster 6.5mms are good choices, and there's nothing wrong with any of the .300 magnums.

When I got that long shot at my Yukon ram, I was carrying a big Lazzeroni rifle in the superfast .308 Warbird cartridge, so I was well prepared for such a shot and had confidence I could pull it off. However, when it comes to sheep rifles, there should be a balance between capability and portability. In the Warbird I had all the capability I could ever use—and then some—but I was in extremely steep and rugged mountains, and I'm not sure I will ever carry such a heavy rifle up another sheep mountain.

Jack O'Connor considered the .270 Winchester an ideal sheep rifle. Although the cartridge is 75 years old, it's still ideal for this size game and this kind of hunting. It will reach out to 350 yards and more without difficulty and can be built into a nice, light, easy-to-carry rifle. The various 7mm rifles are also excellent. I have used both the .280 and the 7mm Remington Magnum on sheep hunts, and they're excellent—not necessarily better than the old .270, but just as good. Another great choice is the .270 Weatherby Magnum. It is one of the flattest-shooting of all cartridges, but it still has light recoil and can be housed in a reasonably light rifle.

The only thing that might be better than the cartridges I've mentioned is the new breed of short magnums that can be housed in compact, short-action rifles. These include

Lazzeroni's .284 Tomahawk and .308 Patriot; Remington's 7mm and .300 Short Action Ultra Mags; and Winchester's family of the .270, 7mm, and .300 Winchester Short Magnum. All of these are fine cartridges, but my pick would be the .270 Winchester Short Magnum because the .270 really is just right for this size game.

Bullet Performance

Our northern sheep are blocky animals but not so large as to require extra-tough bullets. Going back to O'Connor once more, one of his favorite bullets for sheep was the old Remington Bronze Point. Still available, this bullet has a sharp alloy tip that precludes battering in the magazine, improves aerodynamics, and upon impact drives back into the bullet to promote expansion. It is really a forerunner of the modern polymer-tipped bullets—Nosler Ballistic Tip, Winchester Ballistic Silvertip, Hornady SST, Swift Scirocco. These are ideal bullets for hunting our smaller-bodied northern sheep.

You don't want or need extremely tough bullets for any sheep—their body size doesn't call for it. Though you don't want to ruin any more of that tasty meat than is necessary, you definitely don't want your ram to run into the crags where recovery can be difficult. The bullets we have discussed tend to be extremely accurate, but, depending on what works best in your rifle, don't overlook good old conventional softpoints like Sierra GameKing, Hornady Interlock, and tried-and-true factory bullets like Winchester's Power Point, Federal's Hi-Shok, and Remington's Core-Lokt. All offer the relatively rapid expansion you want on this kind of game.

112

Special Circumstances

From British Columbia's Cassiars to the Brooks Range, hunting North America's northern sheep is basically the same from the standpoint of shooting, shot placement, and choice of rifles and cartridges. The wild card, however, is that northern sheep are often hunted in combination with everything from goat to moose, caribou, and even the big bears. Goat rifles and sheep rifles are indistinguishable, and caribou rifles aren't much different. But ideal moose and grizzly bear rifles are probably not ideal sheep rifles. If you are planning a combination hunt, you should choose a rifle and cartridge that are adequate for the largest game but that also have the capability, in terms of accuracy and range, to take your sheep. My first sheep hunt was a combination hunt in northern B.C., and I took my Stone ram with a .375 H&H. It did the job just fine, but it wasn't perfect. Today I would probably take a faster, flatter-shooting magnum on such a hunt, probably a fast .30 if moose were on the agenda and an 8mm Remington Magnum or fast .33 if the hunt included grizzly.

Wolf

For practically all hunters, a wolf skin is a much-sought-after trophy. Take the heart/lung shot to avoid shattering leg bones, which, in turn, tend to cause large exit holes that damage the skin. (Photo courtesy of Len Rue Jr.)

WOLF
Like it or not, the wolf is coming back!

The wolf engenders a deep-seated, atavistic response in many humans. The howl of a wolf in the night brings the hair up on the back of the neck—an unnamed and irrational fear rooted deeply in our prehistoric past. With the urbanization of our society, many have lost this fundamental fear of the wolf, and it is probably they who are clamoring for the wolf's total protection and reintroduction. People of the land, especially farmers and ranchers, take the opposite approach.

There are strong feelings on both sides of the wolf issue. On the one hand, the wolf looks altogether too much like the family dog; on the other hand, it is surrounded by superstition and dread. In reality it is a highly intelligent animal and an efficient predator. The wolf is a threat to wildlife and can be hard on livestock. Wolves are an important part of true wilderness, however, and I think our wild country is much the poorer without their distant howls. On the other hand, there is very little true wilderness that isn't subject to some degree of management by man. The proper position is probably a balanced one. A few wolves are wonderful, but too many wolves can be a serious problem.

Our North American wolf is properly the gray wolf, *Canis lupus*, also called timber wolf and tundra wolf. Although many generally indistinct subspecies have been identified, our wolf is really the same animal as the wolf of Europe and Asia. *Canis lupus* is the largest wild

Wolves almost always are trophies of opportunity during a hunt in Canada or Alaska. Because of this, the hunter will be equipped with a caliber suitable for moose, sheep, bear, or caribou. What is suitable for these animals will do well for a wolf, too. (Photo courtesy of Len Rue Jr.)

Wolf

member of the dog family and is almost certainly the ancestor of our domestic dog. Gray is the most common color, but wolf range from pure white to pure black, with innumerable shades of gray and brown in-between. Most packs have individuals of various colors. The lighter shades are common in the north, and darker wolf are common in the southern parts of their range. The wolf stands about thirty-two inches high at the shoulder, with full-grown males running about 80 to 120 pounds—but outsized specimens can weigh 150 pounds or more.

Until quite recently the wolf has been trapped, poisoned, and shot on sight—and it survived in spite of our best (or worst) efforts. Today, in some Canadian provinces and in Alaska, it is hunted in accordance with seasons, under a big-game tag or a furbearer license. Either way, it genuinely deserves the status it has attained as a full-fledged big-game animal. In fact, by any standard and ethical fair-chase method of hunting, there are very few animals in the world as difficult to hunt as the wolf! The Boone and Crockett record book does not recognize the wolf as a big-game animal, but Safari Club International's record book does.

Shots at Wolf

Today most wolf are taken incidental to hunts for other species. Wolf are present throughout most hunting areas in western Canada and Alaska, so you might encounter a wolf at any time. If the season is open, it's foolish not to have a wolf tag in your pocket. It's very difficult to plan an encounter, but under Murphy's Law, it's almost certain that if you don't have a wolf tag or if the season isn't open, you'll see them all over the place!

The Perfect Shot: Mini Edition for North America II

Along with a wolf tag, a good, loud varmint call is another good item to put into a daypack. Wolf will also come to winter-killed carcasses and the remains of hunter-killed game. In areas where black bear are baited, wolf may also come to bait piles. These encounters are hard to plan and require luck—but this is probably the best way to get a good shot at a wolf. When returning to any downed game, wilderness hunters use extreme caution to avoid encounters with bear, but if you desire a wolf, the best approach is to try to view the carcass from a distance. It isn't easy to sneak up on a wolf even if it's on a kill, but it can be done.

Chance encounters are just that—they are almost impossible to predict, and they can take any form. Typically, wolf hunt along the edges of rivers and streams, and they follow the glacial streambeds when moving from one area to another. These are the most likely areas for a meeting engagement. I know a number of hunters who, over the course of several hunts in Canada and Alaska, have taken more than one wolf.

These days, when the wolf is elevated to big-game status in many hunters' minds, there is a growing market for midwinter wolf hunts. Under some circumstances Alaska's prohibition against "same-day airborne" hunting didn't apply to wolf, so until fairly recently a common hunting technique was to search for wolf from the air, then shadow the pack until the hunters reached a safe place to land on snow skis, and jump out and shoot. Hunters no longer do this, but they conduct some midwinter wolf hunts on snowmobiles in the far north. This is an extremely cold and difficult endeavor. They follow tracks until they find a pack, and then they jump off the snowmobiles and shoot.

Wolf

This means that the shot will be a difficult attempt at a fast-moving target, while the shooter is bundled in multiple layers of bulky clothing. But here's the deal: A shot at a wolf is so difficult to obtain and so rare an opportunity that any shot at a wolf is a great opportunity. If you spot a wolf on a kill and can make a concealed approach, you might get a very simple shot, but most shots at wolf are difficult, either at long range or at a moving animal, or both.

Taking the Shot

The wolf is an extremely intelligent animal, with the keen eyes, excellent ears, and sensitive nose common to all canines. After centuries of attempted extermination, it is ingrained in them that humans are bad news. Whether through luck or skill, if you can get past these defenses and get a shot within reasonable range, you have done well. Wolf are extremely tough animals. On the hunt they run many miles daily, so a healthy wolf is in great physical condition. A wolf can and will travel far and fast with a bad hit, so if you get that rare opportunity to take a wolf, you must hit it well. The chest cavity is the largest vital target, so that is your aiming point—but, if at all possible, go a step further and try to break its shoulder en route to the heart.

The Right Wolf

Safari Club International accepts wolf trophies based on skull measurements, but the real trophy to most hunters is its luxurious hide. Either way, opportunities to take wolf are so rare that it's ridiculous to speak in terms of trophy quality. Any legally taken wolf is a great trophy. Period.

Guns and Loads

Given a choice, the right rifle is probably an accurate, flat-shooting rifle chambered to anything from .243 to one of the .300 magnums. Obviously, it should be scoped, but there is one other criterion that is extremely important: The rifle should fit you well and you should know it well because the only shot you get may well be a running shot. The snow-machine hunters generally use semiautomatic .223s, like the Ruger Mini-14, also a favored gun during the days of fly-and-shoot wolf hunting. This is somewhat opposed to my idea of the right rifle, but running shots are all you get under these circumstances, so I understand where they're coming from. Just remember that since most wolf are taken incidental to hunting other species, the right rifle is probably whatever you have in your hands—if it makes the shot possible.

Bullet Performance

As is often the case, this is far more important than choice of caliber. I'll give you one of my wolf stories. Guide Jack Ringus and I were camped along a river in southeastern Alaska, hunting for bear. It was late in the afternoon, and we were glassing from camp when a lone wolf came trotting along the far bank, maybe 225 yards away. I grabbed my .300 magnum and got into a sitting position, hoping it would stop. Instead, it saw us and sped up. Still, it was the chance of a lifetime. I got the cross hairs on it and swung in front of it, and when the rifle went off, I knew I had it.

Almost. I hit it hard, somewhere in the front quarter, but it got into the thick conifers just up from the riverbank. We got into our waders and crossed the river, easily picking up the spoor. It was hands and knees in thick vegetation, but we could follow the trail. Two or three times we heard the wolf moving in front of us, but eventually it got too dark to follow. No problem—I was sure we'd find it in the morning. Except that it rained hard that night, and we never found another trace.

Now, it should be obvious that a .300 magnum is plenty of gun for this size animal. This being the case, it should be equally obvious that I didn't hit it exactly right. But the wolf was more or less broadside, and the tracks indicated that the on-side foreleg was broken high. So I wasn't very far off! When an animal is lost, you never know exactly what transpired, and it's altogether too easy to blame the bullet. But I was using a tough, deep-penetrating Barnes X-Bullet, just right for the bear I intended to shoot but perhaps a bit too tough for a slender animal the size of a wolf. Perhaps I'm wrong, but to this day I believe I would have a wolf rug in my den had I been using a bullet that had opened up more quickly and done more damage to the animal's vitals. Anyway, it was a sad chapter that still bothers me. When I go on a specific wolf hunt (and I will), I will load up with a faster-opening bullet like a Nosler Ballistic Tip or a Sierra GameKing.